F/O. E.A. DEVERILL. D.F.M.   97 SQUADRON

Flying Officer Ernest Deverill drawn by the war artist Cuthbert Orde in 1942

PATH TO COURAGE

LIFE AND DUTY
OF AN RAF PILOT

MICHAEL STRUTT

TEASEL

PATH TO COURAGE

LIFE AND DUTY OF AN RAF PILOT

MICHAEL STRUTT

ISBN 978-1-7396307-0-6
A CIP catalogue record for this book is available from the British Library

Published 2022 Teasel Books
PO Box 110
Downham Market
Norfolk PE38 8DU

Printed & bound in the UK

CONTENTS

FOREWORD

By Air Marshal C R Spink CB, CBE, RAF Rtd.

There are countless stories that emanate from the Second World War, but in chancing upon an almost forgotten memorial, Michael Strutt has uncovered the path of a true hero. With journalistic zeal, he has followed the life of Ernest Deverill from his formative days through to the savage skies over Europe in the dark days of the 1940s. In doing so, he has not only thrown into sharp relief the extreme dangers of flying in such an unforgiving arena, but has also shown so much of this brave man outside of the cockpit.

The social fabric of this country and the educational system that were such an important part of the young Deverill's life are fascinating, not least the challenge for any young man to make his way in the class structure that was so prevalent at the time. To read of Ernest Deverill's time in the RAF Apprentice scheme, in a period when this was to become such a foundation stone in the building of the Royal Air Force, reminded me of how important this was to those of us who followed on many decades later.

As a boy of 16 years, for boy I still was, I also joined the Royal Air Force as an apprentice from what could be described as a modest background. Like Ernest Deverill I was to go on to pilot training, but from there further parallels cannot be made, because he was thrust into a conflict that would claim many thousands of lives.

He was also flying at a time when aircraft were still very

rudimentary and were being developed and effectively tested in combat. Surviving training was a challenge in itself, and then, in the early days of the war, he flew against the enemy in machines that were frankly outdated and inadequate.

New aircraft did arrive eventually and then new tactics were required to fit them for the many tasks, and again, Deverill was central to this challenge. However, improved as these new aircraft were, they still had systems that were basic by today's standards, and that brought into sharp focus the additional significant danger – the weather.

This is a wonderfully compelling book in which we truly see Ernest Deverill rise from what, at the time, would be described as ordinary beginnings to do quite extraordinary things. We see a man, like so many others, attempting to lead a normal family life while nightly having to show courage of the highest order – not just in one action but night after night after night.

Squadron Leader Ernest Deverill DFC and Bar, AFC, DFM, RAF may have come from ordinary beginnings, but he was no ordinary man. Michael Strutt's narrative is not just about true courage in war, but is an insightful commentary on the social fabric of that time and I commend the book to you.

Cliff Spink
Keyston,
December 2021

INTRODUCTION

This book began with a walk in a churchyard in the village of Docking in Norfolk, eastern England. The walk was organised by Docking Heritage Group members after they had deciphered the faded inscriptions on old graves to produce a plan listing the names of everyone buried there.

On that walk I noticed the grave of a Royal Air Force pilot. The awards he had won, inscribed on the headstone, indicated extraordinary achievements in WWII. I decided to discover more about him.

I found that Squadron Leader Deverill had not only been highly regarded in Bomber Command but also cited in the press for his successful and dangerous flying missions. Unlike most WWII pilots he was already an experienced pilot when war broke out in 1939, having enlisted in the RAF as an apprentice much earlier.

He joined at a time when the air force was a small peacetime organisation with an uncertain future. It was also a time when pilots and officers were recruited mainly from upper-class backgrounds rather than his but the RAF had clearly recognised his special abilities.

I have felt privileged researching Ernest Deverill's eventful life and times. In an era of technological and political change, and personal danger in wartime, Deverill made his mark with skill, grit, bravery and modesty that equals many of his better-known contemporaries who are spoken of as war heroes.

In writing this book I am deeply grateful for the

recollections, records and writings of others, and have sought to make clear where I am expressing my own views. I do not have a time machine but when I turn these pages I find myself in Ernest Deverill's world. As you read this book I hope you are willing to enter that world too.

Michael Strutt
Norfolk,
March 2022

FACE OF A FLIER

The war artist works steadily at his drawing in the winter light of February coming through the window. His subject, a Flying Officer of the Royal Air Force in blue-grey tunic. The officer wears the purple-and-white striped ribbon of the Distinguished Flying Medal (DFM) beneath his RAF wings. It is shortly after his 26th birthday in 1942.

This, one of a series of portraits commissioned by the Air Ministry in London, would take the artist, Cuthbert Orde, about two hours to do. He drew with charcoal as usual, adding highlights in white chalk, and liked to chat with his subject while drawing. As he once explained about his work: "We talked nearly all the time and almost always about flying or about chaps whom we both knew."

A distinguished-looking man in his mid-fifties, Orde knew a lot of chaps and a lot of women. He moved in high social circles, not least through having married in 1916 – as the Great War dragged to its third year – Lady Eileen Wellesley, "the younger of the Duke and Duchess of Wellington's handsome daughters".

Eileen's parents disapproved of the marriage, scenting "its whiff of Bohemia", as she also was an artist – a painter and designer in London's fashion set. By then she also had worked for two years as a nurse in a London hospital for wounded soldiers from the Western Front; some nurses and patients from the hospital were wedding guests.

Like his sitter, Cuthbert Orde had been an airman, serving in France as an observer then pilot in the Royal Flying Corps, with promotion from Lieutenant to Captain.

During the 1920s and 30s Captain Orde pursued a career as still-life artist and portrait painter to London society, with his pictures shown at Royal Society of Portrait Painters exhibitions, the Royal Academy, private galleries in London and the Paris Salon.

His work was turned down on more than one occasion, to his annoyance. "Cuthbert is always starting a new picture, like the labours of Sisyphus," the writer Stella Benson – one of his sitters and friend of the Ordes – noted in her diary in December 1928. By then, remarkably, Eileen was painting by holding the brush in her mouth, because of tremors from a chronic condition.

The couple, keen poker players who shared a racy sense of humour, had embraced "a new, anything goes, style of London social life" – as Benson described it – in the aftermath of the war. They dined with friends at the fashionable French restaurant Boulestin, in Covent Garden, opened by the renowned chef Marcel Boulestin. The decoration included "very large, and extremely modern, mural paintings" with a circus theme.

At night, Cuthbert and Eileen turned up at bohemian parties. And they frequented Soho's raffish Gargoyle Club, "a rooftoop den reached by a rickety lift" where the wealthy and titled danced, dined, and mixed with (rather less well-heeled) artists, writers and poets.

The hand-picked membership, the theatrical décor that included two paintings by Henri Matisse, created "a world of expectancy", one member recalled. The Gargoyle was a place where unconventional people like the Ordes could be free of upper-class convention.

After war came again, in September 1939, Cuthbert Orde was one of many artists who applied to the newly formed War Artists Advisory Committee to offer their services – not least because the flow of commissions had dwindled. During the hectic months of the Battle of Britain in 1940, as the country faced invasion, he and Eric Kennington drew or painted hundreds of fighter pilots and other RAF men, travelling "all over the place" as Orde put it in a letter to the committee.

He spent about ten days at a time at aerodromes up and down the country. The frequent change of location made him write asking that cheques for his pictures should be paid straight to his bank.

Many of these head-and-shoulders drawings were made at forward airfields in makeshift studios "generally set up in the ladies' room in the mess". Often he worked while an officer (less often, a sergeant pilot) waited in flying kit to scramble at a moment's notice in a Spitfire or Hurricane; or had landed after combat.

Orde was enthusiastic about his work, keen to portray the character of these airmen. It was said that "Turps" Orde[1], or simply "The Captain", had "the happy knack of being able to mix with the youngest pilot officer on level terms and gain their confidence and friendship".

He would do perhaps two drawings in a morning, continue in the afternoon, then mix in the officers mess that evening, sharing "their frequent and hilarious parties". Carrying out further commissions for the Air Ministry in 1941 he surprised one of his sitters, a fighter pilot, by saying: "I've left room for the DFC. The people I draw always seem to get it." The pilot did – four days later.

So here, on a day in early 1942, the officer's features emerge steadily on Orde's sheet of toned paper: nose, eyes, mouth, neatly combed dark hair. The conversation is friendly; Orde liked to joke but he is quietly observing his subject, drawing on years of craft painting the well-connected, Winston Churchill among them, without any need to flatter his subject. As he explained once with a certain modesty: "There is a saying, it takes two to make a portrait, and each must work his hardest."

The officer, meanwhile, appears to be observing the artist as he works. He is looking intently, or perhaps feels he is there out of duty – given he was picked for the task to satisfy the Air Ministry, by his Group or station commander. His expression and pose, as Orde steadily records it, reveal what may not be said in words: like many airmen fighting the war this pilot has had many a "shaky do".

Some of his flying experiences since 1939 have been hair-raising: from dangerously unreliable aeroplanes to sorties where luck more than his considerable flying skills kept him alive. More than once he has flown a shot-up machine home and walked away from the crash-landing, though not all his crewmen have been so fortunate.

The finished picture is compelling. The head is fully drawn, the tunic, pilot's wings and medal ribbon only loosely suggested; but not as an afterthought, the focus is entirely on the subject's bearing and expression. He looks out at the viewer with a steady, unnerving gaze, his hooded eyes expressing readiness, wariness.

Rather than the "good likeness" this pilot might have expected it is a penetrating study. Revealed in the dark tones, the varied strokes of charcoal, are character, sense of purpose and personal responsibility. It is the portrait of a man who has seen much, perhaps too much.

As the sitting ends the artist prints in capitals under the picture F/O E. A. Deverill DFM plus his squadron. He signs it in capitals *ORDE* with a casual sweep, adding the date.

His fee, about five guineas[2], will be paid, eventually,

after this picture with others he delivers is considered and, he hopes, approved for purchase.

Another session wrapped up. Yet who is the pilot chosen to sit for him? What act of flying earned the airman his DFM award? What path took him into the RAF and pushed him forward to have his portrait drawn in this, the third year of the war?

Winding backwards in time, his path encompasses many things. The progress of the war of course, but before that – childhood – education – and ambition.

THE KING'S SHIPS

Ernest Alfred Deverill was born on February 2 1916 in a modest terraced house in Balmoral Road, Gillingham, north Kent. His parents, Ernest Arthur and Alice Maude Deverill (always known as "Elsie"), had married in 1913 and Ernest was the first of their three children.

Both his parents were from London families. His father was born in Highbury, north London in 1888 as the son of a gas fitter. Elsie (née Keeble) came from Poplar in the overcrowded East End by the London docks.

Her parents were fortunate to live in Grosvenor Buildings, where her father was the superintendent/caretaker. This was a huge new development of more than 500 "model homes" built on the site of slums. Each flat had piped running water and its own inside lavatory – facilities that many families in the East End did not have.

The Deverills and the Keebles had a strong service background on both sides. In 1916 Ernest's father was in the Royal Navy; during the war his four brothers all served in the Army, in France, India, Mesopotamia and Egypt. All returned unscathed. On Elsie's side were soldiers and policemen.

Gillingham, on the estuary of the River Medway, was a working town whose fortunes were tied to the Navy dockyard at Chatham nearby. In the history books Gillingham had made its mark for two other reasons. It was the birthplace of William Adams, an adventurous seaman who in April 1600 was the first Englishman to land in Japan, where he became adviser to a Shogun ruler.

A few years later, during the Dutch war with England, Gillingham was the scene of an audacious attack by the Dutch fleet. Sailing into the Medway, the raiders breached an iron security chain across the river to "where the King's ships do lie" moored and unmanned, and set some ablaze. Adding to the humiliation, two vessels, one the flagship *Royal Charles*, were captured and towed back to Holland as trophies. There was panic in London.

Ernest and Elsie both were strong characters, forged by their upbringing and experience of life. Elsie was a keen swimmer, taking a dip every day whenever possible. Her husband had joined the Navy at 15 or 16; his experience of the service – that is, the Royal Navy of the early 20th century – had a profound influence on the young Ernest. His father's tough training in the Navy, starting on the bottom rung, equally must have been a profound influence on the family.

Ernest senior, born in 1882, enlisted in the Royal Navy as a Boy Entrant, with his parents' permission, having worked as a clerk after leaving school. His initial training was on *Impregnable*, the three-masted wooden hulk moored at Devonport.

The regime on *Impregnable* was a common introduction to the Navy's methods: boys learned to sleep in a hammock and the ways of living on a Navy ship. Discipline was harsh and the food poor; the decks were scrubbed clean early each day in almost any weather.

Seamanship skills were taught in strict accordance with the Navy's *Manual of Seamanship*. These included knotting and splicing ropes, ships' rigging, signalling using flags and ensigns, Morse code, and semaphore, plus the all-important training in boat work.

Boat work was the whole range of disciplines to sail

and "pull" (the Navy word for rowing) the various craft, up to 45 feet long, carried by Navy ships. This training was a formative experience in itself. Ships' boats included launches, dinghies, gigs and steam cutters, but in particular the versatile 25 and 27-foot whalers and 32-foot cutters.

Cutters and whalers (pulling five up to 12 oars) were the open boats used at sea since Nelson's day for general tasks such as rescue, transferring officers between ships, to board vessels in war, for running mail. A good soaking was likely while manoeuvring in a rough sea.

Optimum efficiency in pulling was essential. The manual said: "What is required is to aim at getting freedom of joints, supple muscles, limbs and brain acting conjointly, and lungs acting freely."[3]

Boy entrants were drilled relentlessly by the instructors until their boat work was faultless, pushing them to the limit in exercises and ferocious "obstacle races". They learned to switch from oars to sail, and back again, in seconds.

These skills had to be perfected both on the water and while lowering and hoisting the boats. To fall short during the exercises earned an instant *thwhack* from the instructor's cane, or his *stonnachie* – a rope's end.

Ernest Deverill qualified as a Boy Seaman 1st Class and, on his 18th birthday in 1906, signed up for 12 years. Boy seamen were "at everybody's beck and call", including putting their backs into coaling duties in port.

A naval cadet wrote: "Coal-burning ships… had a peculiar camaraderie and discipline based on hard physical labour. When we took on coal, every last man (including the so-called idlers such as the chaplain, paymaster and major of marines) was put to work shovelling coal, stropping up bags for the hoist, wheeling barrows, trimming coal in the bunkers. Woe betide any man who shirked his fair share of the work!"[4]

It was an extraordinary time for a young man to join the world's most powerful navy, steeped in the Nelson tradition. In the top echelons the service was impossibly grand. For ceremonial occasions their Lordships the Sea Lords, who sat on the Admiralty Board, wore flamboyant 18th century-style uniforms festooned with gold braiding and showy epaulettes, topped by a cocked hat. Yet, tradition aside, the Navy was engaged in an extended period of radical change.

In 1880, by which time steam-powered warships had replaced wooden sailing ships, the service opened its own college to train the engineering officers required to manage the increasingly specialist machinery and electrical equipment such as gunnery rangefinders.

In 1903 the Admiralty declared an end to training for sail, bringing in "physical and mechanical training", to build a modern technical force. Around the time Boy Seaman Deverill signed up, pay and food were improved with bread baked daily on board in place of the traditional dry ship's biscuits. However, for reasons of discipline, tradition and pride, the skills and turnout of boat crews were maintained, and fostered through inter-ship competitions. "A ship is known by its boats", the Navy said.

The symbol of this modernisation programme was a new kind of battleship, *Dreadnought*, launched in 1906. It was the first of a revolutionary class of steel warships powered by steam turbines in place of the well-tried triple-expansion steam engines.

Stark and menacing in its grey paint, *Dreadnought* carried a blistering main armament of ten 12-inch guns mounted in five turrets, directed by a centralised fire-control system. This gave the Navy concentrated firepower at a range of more than 20,000 yards (about 11 miles).

The admirals were eyeing a growing German fleet but *Dreadnought*-class ships heralded a British navy that could win the big sea battles they envisaged. These ships would be powered in future by cleaner, more-economical fuel oil instead of coal. However a decade later, in the Great War, Portsmouth's huge naval barracks still housed thousands of stokers required to shovel coal into the boilers at sea, in sweltering engine rooms.

As for many Navy men from an ordinary background, Seaman Deverill's suitability for promotion was thanks in great part to an important piece of legislation, the 1870 Education Act. The Act was passed "to provide a system… which shall penetrate the length and breadth of the land, and as quickly as possible bring within the reach of every child in England and Wales the means of learning reading, writing, and arithmetic."

Backed by a second Act in 1880, State education to age ten was made compulsory; the school-leaving age rose to 11 in 1893 and 12 in 1899. So Ernest Deverill senior was born at the right time as, until the late 19th century, the Navy had many seamen who could not read or write.

Life on the Navy's "lower deck", out of sight of the commissioned officers with their privileges, remained harsh into the next century. Obstacles persisted for those on the lower deck to be commissioned. Families of the middle and upper classes used their good connections to ensure that their well-educated sons, joining as cadets, filled the commissions once they passed increasingly technical exams.

However, the Navy of necessity was beginning to make changes to remedy an unfair system. Its commanders looked for capabilities in the men below deck and noted comments on their record to steer them into training as skilled ratings and potential officers. From Seaman, Ernest Deverill earned regular favourable reports over the years – "Tactful and conscientious", "Competent, zealous, energetic, experienced" said two of these as, gradually, he was promoted.

A Leading Seaman in 1914 – and married – he was sent on a 50-day course at the "stone frigate" *HMS Vernon*, the Navy's onshore torpedo and ordnance school in Portsmouth. This course gave ratings a thorough knowledge of gun and fire-control equipment, lighting circuitry and dynamos, as well as the workings of torpedoes and their gyroscopes.

Passing the course gained him the rating Gunner (T) – torpedoes – by which he entered the Engineering Branch of the service. He reached the rank of Petty Officer [Warrant] during the war, serving on two battleships.

He continued his naval career after the war. By 1920 he and Elsie had a second son, Derek, and a daughter, Doreen. But Navy life in peacetime did not stand still and four years on it brought a big change for the family.

ACROSS THE WORLD

On November 29 1923 Ernest's ship, the sleek D-Class cruiser *Dunedin* (6-inch guns and a complement of 450 men) sailed from Devonport as part of a Special Service Squadron making a round-the-world tour. The 10-month voyage was publicised by the Admiralty as the "World Cruise", a goodwill tour by seven warships. They would call at many ports: in Africa, the Far East, Australia and New Zealand, South America, Canada and the United States.

The flagship for this voyage was the world's biggest warship "the mighty *Hood*". So the cruise, with a total complement of 4,600 personnel, was a demonstration of Britain's sea power – a reminder to all that the Royal Navy still ruled the seas.

Not all the ships would carry out the full tour. *Dunedin*, with Petty Officer Deverill among her crew, would stay behind in New Zealand with a second cruiser, *Diomede*, to be attached to the New Zealand Division of the Royal Navy.

The squadron crossed the Equator on December 14 (each seaman was given a crossing-the-line certificate) then called at ports in countries that had aided Britain during the war: Freetown in Sierra Leone, Cape Town, Zanzibar, Trincomalee in Ceylon, and Singapore.

The arrivals were welcomed with parades, functions, events, sailors were taken on excursions. Thousands went aboard the *Hood* for "At Home" visits. For the crews it was the trip of a lifetime, the "World Booze" as they joked on the mess decks.

Reaching Australia, the squadron stayed a week in Melbourne where a sporting festival was held. Football, cricket and boxing teams from the ships gave a good account of themselves ashore against Australian teams; while more than 200,000 people visited the *Hood*. Crowds of "half a million people lined Sydney harbour to watch the Squadron glide in on April 9".[5] By this time, for many sailors, the novelty, and work required at each stop, was wearing thin. A number of them had jumped ship.

The squadron arrived in Auckland, in the North Island of New Zealand, on May 22 1924. *Dunedin* and *Diomede* were transferred to strengthen the country's fledgling Navy, making Deverill a serviceman of the New Zealand Navy.

The compact city of Auckland, with its two huge natural harbours, was situated amid spectacular vistas of coastline and water. The naval base at Devonport, on the city outskirts, was small. It had no wardroom with living quarters, so the personnel lived out in the surrounding district.

Dunedin's main duties comprised voyages 1,500 miles north to visit the islands of Western Samoa, for which New Zealand, as part of the British Empire, had held powers of administration under international mandate since 1914. There would be visits to ports in New Zealand and Australia.

After carrying out sea trials, in June *Dunedin* sailed and began calling at an extraordinary variety of scattered islands: Vava'u, Pago Pago, Niue, Rarotonga, Suva, Sunday Island, Kekuva. These remote places, those inhabited and others uninhabited, appeared at first sight to be a paradise of sun-drenched beaches and lush vegetation.

However, all was not well among the communities

living there. The Polynesian culture, and Polynesians' growing resentment against colonial rule, was poorly understood by the politicians far away in Wellington. A modern report explains:

New Zealand was ill-equipped to cope with the Samoa mandate. It had no formal foreign service, so officials were seconded to Samoa from New Zealand's public service. Few stayed on for more than one three-year term, or took the time to learn the language or fully understand the culture.[6]

Forceful methods were used by the government in Wellington to change the Samoans' culture of social organisation, of songs, myths and legends, to fit the European view – insisting on formal schooling and that villages should be neatly laid out. But this policy was being actively resisted. The splash of an anchor as a navy ship hove to off a beautiful beach, with Marines available to enforce the government will, carried a message.

Ernest senior and Elsie were now on opposite sides of the world but there was a practical outcome: the Navy arranged for the family to join him in Auckland. Young Ernest was now eight, Derek five and Doreen three.

They sailed from Southampton on September 26 1924 on the steamship *Tainui*, a passenger/cargo vessel of the Shaw Savill Line making the regular New Zealand run via the Panama Canal. Other passengers on the five-week voyage included a wool buyer, farmer, engineer and a lady's maid. Divine Service was held on Sunday mornings for those who wished to attend.

Crossing the Pacific Ocean with 3,000 miles still to travel to Auckland, the steamer hove to off a remote speck on the map – Pitcairn Island. From under forbidding cliffs, Pitcairn men rowed out to the ship in their 38-foot longboats through the "tumultuous surf pounding into Botany Bay". Passing ships such as *Tainui* were an opportunity for Pitcairners – descendants of Fletcher Christian, leader of the mutiny on the *Bounty* – to barter the island's abundant fresh fruit for useful goods and sell crafts to the passengers.

In Auckland, during her husband's absences at sea, Elsie managed the young children with the independence common to a sailor's wife. The children will have gone to local schools; and it was probably at Auckland's beaches that young Ernest, his sister and brother, learnt to swim well under the keen eye of their mother.

For the family it was a time of new experiences, particularly since they lived out of the naval base. And they would have encountered the lives of the Maori people because of the plight of this indigenous population. There was an obvious contrast between the ordered ruling society of European stock and conditions of the Maoris. Many lived in visibly crowded, insanitary homes.

Over generations there had been conflict between the two cultures, also assimilation through intermarriage. Maoris had adopted some European ways and fought for the Empire in the Great War. Even so, their colourful arts, ancient myths and customs still held mystical power. Yet in the 1920s the Maori people were struggling to survive. Thousands had died in the flu epidemic of 1918.

In 1924, when the Deverills arrived, the spread of typhoid brought the deaths of many more Maoris. Large numbers were put in isolation camps in remote areas to try to contain the disease.

The government worked with Maori representatives headed by the influential leader Te Puea Herangi, a shrewd, forceful woman who had an English grandfather. They were making increasingly public efforts to tackle the underlying issues, which included living conditions and disputes over land ownership.

After more than three years in Auckland, as the children grew, change came again for the family when Ernest Deverill snr was commissioned and posted back to Britain. This upheaval across the world was a normal part of service life, but he had joined the officer class. And for young Ernest, now aged 12, his brother and sister, the move heralded a different future.

A CITY, A HOME

The steamship *Tamaroa* sailed for England from Auckland on Saturday January 21 1928. Ernest, Elsie and the children travelled together as "saloon passengers" (first class) for the five-week voyage. *Tamaroa* docked in Southampton on February 27 and they went on to Chislehurst, close to London, for a temporary stay.

Ernest senior was based in Portsmouth while on foreign service leave and reverted to the Royal Navy in June. In October he reported to join the staff at *HMS Vernon*, the torpedo training base. And so Portsmouth became the family's home.

They moved into a house in Lichfield Road, Copnor, a northern suburb of comfortable terraced streets near St Mary's Infirmary. Portsmouth was expanding: Copnor had been mostly farmland until recent years and complaints continued in the local newspaper that services remained unfinished as some roads were a quagmire. With fond memories of their time in New Zealand, Ernest and Elsie named their new home *Haeremai*, a Maori greeting meaning welcome.

Portsmouth was the country's biggest naval base, steeped in 1,000 years of history. For centuries it was a heavily fortified garrison town defending England against invasion. In July 1545, Henry VIII watched dismayed from Southsea Castle as his flagship *Mary Rose* capsized and sank in the waters of the Solent.

A walk through the High Street passed The George Hotel, where a wall plaque recorded that Admiral Horatio

Nelson "spent his last hours in England" there in October 1805. From The George one morning, Nelson walked to the beach at Southsea to be rowed out – to cheers from crowds of well-wishers – to his ship *Victory* by the Isle of Wight. From here he sailed to meet his fate off the coast of Spain at the Battle of Trafalgar.

Cheek by jowl in Portsmouth centre, where sailors walked the streets frequenting the public houses and ale houses, stood the main railway station and goods yard, commercial offices, and theatres. Towering above these buildings, the splendid Victorian Guildhall provided some unexpected grandeur. This was in part because the Guildhall, with its classical columns, wide flight of steps and elaborate clock tower, was a close copy of Bolton Town Hall, pride of the Lancashire cotton town and designed by the same architect.

In Commercial Road was "Aggie's", the Royal Sailors' Rest, an institution known throughout the Navy. Its origins were in the 19th century Temperance movement: at Aggie's, footloose sailors ashore could find lodging, recreation facilities and meals in alcohol-free premises, all designed to steer them away from trouble with drink.

Portsmouth, in the 1920s, was unique in being an industrial city on England's South Coast. Almost half the workforce were employed in the naval dockyard. There was also a substantial industry manufacturing clothing, in particular corsets.

The Deverills returned to a country still in desperate straits after the General Strike of 1926. Even in Portsmouth the numbers unemployed were increasing steadily. Portsmouth council was starting to demolish "many wretched little streets" close to the dockyard in a slum-clearance programme, to build new homes.

However the family's return to England was well timed: father was established in his Navy career and the move would settle the children's education. Portsmouth had good schools and was easy to get around using the efficient tram service. It was said that "nearly everybody in Portsmouth was within half a mile of a stop".

Also there was Southsea, between the city centre and the Solent. This middle-class and working class suburb with its mix of shops, Victorian villas and terraced streets, was where many Navy officers lived. Southsea offered the city's population ample opportunities for leisure on their doorstep: the beach, two piers, public houses, theatres, music halls and cinemas.

The new "talking films" began showing in the city soon after the Deverills moved there. "Talkies" were filling the 1,700 seats in Southsea's impressive Plaza cinema.

The promenade and piers in Southsea had attracted the genteel class of holiday visitor since Victorian times but, in 1923, Portsmouth council purchased the huge expanse of Southsea Common from the War Office. In a burst of civic energy it was transformed from "a bare waste" of marshy grass and shingle.

By 1928, the council had installed flower beds, tennis courts and bowling greens, a bandstand, boating lake, and miniature steam railway. An ambitious rock garden was planned that would have water features and sub-tropical plants.

Beside the promenade walk between Clarence Pier and Southsea Castle stood the tall Portland stone obelisk of the Royal Naval War Memorial, unveiled in 1924. This commemorated almost 10,000 men of the Portsmouth station missing at sea during the Great War, their names listed on the bronze panels around its base.

Southsea's residential streets opened on to the seafront in a dramatic panorama, the waters of the Solent busy with small craft, ferries and large ships. Ocean liners steamed into and from Southampton.

Among the Navy ships passing, and symbolising the service, was "the mighty *Hood*". On a fine day the view from the promenade was a stirring sight.

WHAT HURTS, TEACHES

Settling in Portsmouth, Elsie and her husband put the children into new schools. Ernest and Derek (always called "Dimps" in the family), aged 12 and nine, were enrolled at one of the best-known boys' secondary schools, Esplanade House in Southsea. The children's new life opened up the possibilities of competitive swimming and all three became members of the city's Northsea Swimming Club.

Esplanade House School, called "Chivers" for short (after the former principal William Chivers), was on the far side of town from Copnor, a ride on the number 7 tram to get there, number 8 to return. This private school was a "crammer" offering a rigorous grammar school-level education for boys from a modest background, for which it charged about £3 per term. Boys wore a uniform comprising a grey jacket, trousers and cap, white shirt and red-and-black striped tie.

The school occupied a tall brick building, with gas lighting, behind a high wall in Cottage Grove. It had earned its reputation over more than 50 years for successes in preparing pupils for government examinations. Boys took these exams to win places in the Civil Service clerical branch, apprenticeships in naval dockyards, or to become an engine-room artificer ("tiffy"), the most highly trained engineers on Royal Navy ships.

To train as a "tiffy" was "the in thing to aim for" at Chivers, so those who went into the Senior Service found "there was a saying: 'There is hardly a wardroom in the Navy that hasn't got an ex-Chivers boy in it'."

Meanwhile, the newest exam, run by the Air Ministry in London, enabled boys nominated by their headmaster to the local education authority to compete for technical apprenticeships in the Royal Air Force. The RAF in 1928 was just ten years old.

This was an education that would test young Ernest's abilities and more besides. The school's principal, John Tribe, a member of the Royal Society of Teachers and former star pupil, had taken over from William Chivers himself. He was a commanding presence, his moustache bristling when he was disconcerted by the boys' behaviour. The three principal masters working with him were all very capable teachers who, it was recalled, often deputised for each other in the various subjects.

The school's records of that time have been lost, but former pupils vividly remembered their days at this unusual institution. One of these boys, TE Wooden, was at Chivers not long after Ernest and taught by the same masters.

There were three classrooms, he recalled. In the ground-floor Little Room the 30 youngest boys and newcomers were taught the basics of arithmetic, algebra and English grammar. The Dockyard Room, on the same floor, had 40 or more pupils.

The third classroom, up a steep worn stairway, "was a daunting affair with its 80-plus pupils of varying ages and scholastic achievement in one large lofty room". Its ceiling was festooned with countless nib pens and long-dried blobs of blotting paper, flicked up there by generations of boys sitting at the well-worn desks below. "In windy, wet weather those sitting under the ventilator lantern were subjected to a spray of droplets and water driven through the lantern slats."[7]

In this room boys were chosen, one at a time, to step on to the rostrum and explain one of Euclid's theorems to the whole class from memory, while chalking the geometry on the blackboard. They were expected to speak up loudly so all could take notes; if done successfully the boy had to explain another theorem.

"But the difference between Chivers and other schools", said another ex-pupil, "was that 'talking in class' was not an idle matter. The boys were discussing their work. The headmaster let them carry on until the din became so terrific that he would thunder: '*Silence!*'"[8]

In an era when pupils were addressed by their surname, corporal punishment was widely believed to be a necessary means to keep order. At Chivers, teaching methods were "a mixture of casualness and strictness, with a liberal use of the cane". The gates were shut when proceedings started at 8am. They were re-opened at nine to let in late pupils, who were caned on the backside by a deputy master as they entered.

The Victorian belief in "spare the rod and spoil the child" was actively pursued through the day until school finished at 4pm. Punishment was the norm whenever boys failed to meet the exacting standards demanded by Mr Tribe and his equally determined deputy masters. One former pupil recalled every boy in his class being caned for a mistake made by one of them.

The school closed at lunchtime. "This allowed the boys to cross the road to buy liquorice sticks, lemonade crystals and ice-creams in the 'tuck shop' opposite," TE Wooden recalled.

There were no sports facilities. The curriculum concentrated closely on subjects required for the exams, in particular English, mathematics, science, history, geography, and drawing. School hours were demanding, from Monday morning to Saturday half-day, plus two compulsory evening sessions from 5-7pm. A pile of homework each evening drove the boys to labour until midnight if necessary in fear of the consequences if they failed to complete it.

The school motto *Quae nocent docent* ("What hurts, teaches"), the title of a poem by Samuel Taylor Coleridge, was a clear reminder to boys and parents alike of Chivers' aims. This poem expresses regret for the opportunities wasted in youth and Mr Tribe was determined that none of his pupils would do the same, using the frequent swish of the cane to get results.

Meanwhile, among the pupils it was believed that the staff were only interested in boys of exceptional ability.

At Christmas the masters briefly revealed a warmer side to their character by hosting a party for the boys at which they provided food and simple entertainment. Mr Tribe impressed with his violin playing, another master gave orations, and a third performed magic.

As well as sitting government exams the pupils took external exams in the national education system. These included the London Matriculation and Oxford School Certificate. The teaching at Chivers was said to be on a par with that at Portsmouth Grammar School. As Chivers intended, it turned out confident, capable young men – taking with them lasting memories of the frequent punishments.

Ernest Deverill proved to be a hardworking pupil and among the school's most able boys: diligent, quick-thinking, with an ability to master maths and science. The Navy, or its dockyards, was the obvious choice for an apprenticeship in which his father's career as a torpedo officer could have steered him, and Derek, in a similar direction. However, by the late 1920s, the glamour of flying had captured the public imagination, and probably Ernest's too.

Britain was becoming increasingly "air-minded", partly by interest in the exploits of British fighter aces such as Ball and McCudden during the 1914-18 War. Flying was being taken up by wealthy people who obtained a pilot's licence. Some country estates had their own airstrip and the annual RAF Air Pageant at Hendon became a social event.

The pageant offered "breathtaking thrills" – formation and aerobatic flying, the latest machines in the aircraft park, and set-piece "battles" with pyrotechnic explosions to demonstrate the RAF's role of "air policing" in far-off parts of the British Empire.

The public fascination with flying may well have fired Ernest with a wish to fly and a career in the RAF, but in peacetime it was a small, cash-strapped service burdened by government cuts to its budget. One man who enlisted in that period recalled: "I don't think many people knew much about it. There was the Hendon air displays but [the RAF] didn't get much publicity."[9]

Meanwhile, high-ups in the Army and Navy continued to lobby for this upstart service to be split up "and returned to its former owners". They sniffed that RAF men were "motor mechanics in uniform".

In summer 1929, an international speed competition came to Portsmouth that was marvelled at, and must have made a big impression on Ernest, then aged 13. The Schneider Trophy Contest for racing seaplanes, declared W E Johns, writer of the Biggles books, was "one of the greatest sporting events in the history of the world".

A FASHIONABLE EVENT

It looked very doubtful that Britain would host the 1929 Schneider Trophy event. The 1927 race, at Venice, was won by Flying Officer Webster of the RAF's High Speed Flight at 281mph in a Supermarine S5.

This victory entitled Britain to host the next contest but the government was not prepared to finance the British entry, which involved the cost of new aircraft.

However, national prestige was at stake. In late 1928 Winston Churchill, Chancellor of the Exchequer, was persuaded to authorise funds to support the High Speed Flight again.

The location for the race would be in the south of England: flying a four-sided course over the Solent between Southsea and the Isle of Wight. Portsmouth council began preparations for one million visitors on race day, among them VIPs, guests of the Royal Navy, and "private flying parties".

To stay competitive, Supermarine switched its engine maker from Napier to Rolls-Royce but by early 1929 development time was short. Weeks of high-power testing at the Rolls works in Derby resulted in a 12-cylinder racing engine producing 1,850hp, and a noisy racket heard across the city.

Race day was set for Saturday September 7. Pilots had to complete seven 50-kilometre laps of near full-power flying, banking round pylons at the four turns. The seafronts at Southsea and Gosport offered two of the best vantage points. At Gosport, stands and enclosures were planned with parking "for 20,000 cars, charabancs and motorcycles".

For the wealthy and well-connected the Schneider was a "must addition" to the social calendar. Shortly after Cowes Week at the beginning of August the *Portsmouth Evening News* told its readers:

"A great many hostesses who have been entertaining for the yachting festival are arranging to return in September to entertain their friends for the great aeroplane contest… Lord and Lady Dorchester are to be host and hostess to a very large party and Mr and Mrs Ernest Guinness, who have so many sporting interests, will have guests not only at their house in Cowes but on their yacht *Fantome*."[10]

The American and French contenders dropped out, leaving Britain and Italy as the only nations to compete. Italy's Macchi machines would race against the Supermarines and Gloster VI planes.

Schneider Trophy Week opened on Monday September 2 in hot sunshine. The Italian and British pilots made their final test flights but Gloster withdrew with unsolved engine problems. Only the three scarlet Macchis and three silver/blue Supermarines, the S5 of 1927 and new S6, were left.

On Friday, the regulations stated, these machines had to pass "seaworthiness trials" on the water "to ensure that the seaplanes entered for the contest are not mere racing freaks".

Flight magazine reported: "Cowes was an important centre for the Schneider Trophy Contest. The roadstead was thronged with gaily decorated yachts and other craft, while *HMS Iron Duke* and the aircraft carrier *Argus* were in prominent positions in the Cowes anchorage." On Saturday, race day, "Southsea woke in the morning to

37

find that its population had doubled during the night, and people were still pouring into the town," one newspaper reported.

"Stands were filled with men in cool flannel suits and women dressed in brilliantly coloured frocks and carrying parasols as some protection against the almost tropical heat and brilliant sun glare. Thousands of picnic parties were seen along the miles of front."[11]

By lunchtime, Southsea promenade and beach were packed to the water's edge. Could the Deverill family, with a picnic, be spotted among the crowds?

The starting gun fired at 2pm, each aircraft being timed from Ryde pier at 15-minute intervals. At 200 feet or less the aircraft streaked down the Solent, banking near-vertically at the turns.

The final scoreboard showed Flying Officer Waghorn (S6) the winner, at a phenomenal average speed of 328.63mph. Warrant Officer Molin of Italy (Macchi M52R) was second at 284.20mph; Flight Lieutenant D'Arcy Greig (S5) third at 282.11mph.

Flying Officer Atcherley (S6) finished at 325.54mph but was disqualified for passing inside a pylon. The Italian pilots Cadringher and Monti both dropped out on the second lap with overheated engines.

So Britain retained the Schneider Trophy until 1931. As WE Johns wrote in *The Modern Boy's Book of Aircraft*: "Those fortunate enough to witness the spectacle of the projectile-like machines hurtling through the air to the powerful roar of those wonderful engines are never likely to forget it."

MAKING THE CHOICE

In January 1931, as the new term started at Chivers, Ernest Deverill approached his 15th birthday with examinations looming that spring. He was entered for all three apprentice competitions: Navy artificer, dockyard apprentice and RAF apprentice, plus at least two Junior Oxford exams. Derek, being younger, would sit his another year. Meanwhile, Doreen, at ten, was collecting an impressive number of swimming cups won in school and city events.

Ernest had a great deal of work to get through in those last few months at Chivers. The former pupil TE Wooden believed the boys were expected to take as many exams as possible, so that high scores reflected well on the school. As for the RAF exam, in late January the Air Ministry announced the national competition for the second of that year's two intakes of apprentices, with 500 places available.

Newspaper reports said: "The scheme offers a good opportunity for well-educated boys of obtaining a three years' apprentice course of a high standard and of following an interesting technical career." Boys had to be aged 15 to 17 and of "pure European descent".

Trades open to them included metal rigger, "a new trade brought into existence by the introduction of the metal aeroplane, which involves training in both fitting and sheet-metal work". Also, fitter (aero engine); fitter (armourer); wireless operator/mechanic; and instrument maker.

"Successful candidates will be required to complete 12 years of regular Air Force service from the age of 18, in addition to the training period", the announcement said.

After completing his apprenticeship, an aircraftman could be considered for training as a pilot once he had served on a unit for a year. When the course ended, up to three apprentices could be awarded a cadetship to learn to fly at the RAF College, Cranwell.

An Air Ministry pamphlet assured parents that their sons would be in good hands: "Apprentices are accommodated separately from men" and "their health and general welfare are given careful and continuous supervision". They were "not allowed to drink intoxicating liquors" and special attention was given to physical training with "ample opportunities for games and exercise in the open air".[12]

The RAF's emphasis on health and welfare may have been a lesson learned from the Army's experience in the 1914-18 War. Many men from lower-class families were found to be in poor physical shape when conscription was brought in in 1916. An item in *The Times* noted that because of the state of the men's teeth the Army had to employ 500 extra dentists.

The exams period was April to June. The RAF exam was held on June 2 with Portsmouth being one of the examining centres. For this Ernest had to complete four papers – Mathematics, Science, a General paper, and English composition with an emphasis on spelling. Among the calculations asked for in the maths paper were – perhaps not surprisingly – "Properties of angles, triangles, quadrilaterals, circles, loci" – i.e., the substance of Euclid's theorems.

When the exam results were published Chivers'

placings were impressive once more, not least in the RAF competition. The Air Ministry stated that 380 of the 1,463 candidates were successful. "E. A. Deverill" was placed fourth. Chivers proudly announced in the local papers: "Five of the first eight successful candidates were prepared by Mr J A Tribe and staff of Esplanade House School."

Ernest was one of several boys from the school who scored full marks for the RAF maths paper. In the artificer apprentice exam, he came 12th out of 379 successful candidates who competed for 58 places. And he came 14th out of 215 candidates for 80 dockyard places.[13] His performance in the Junior Oxford exams was also outstanding: First Class Honours with Distinction in Mathematics and Art.

The letter from the Air Ministry that set Ernest's future course was addressed to his parents. Their son, it said, was accepted for entry as an apprentice "subject to his passing the Royal Air Force medical examination and other conditions" at induction. A following letter enclosed a rail warrant to travel to Marylebone station in London, for a special train to the No.1 School of Technical Training at RAF Halton, in Buckinghamshire. "As each boy will receive a complete outfit on entry, he should not be provided on joining with more than he is likely to need for the first fortnight of the course," the letter said.

Despite Britain's increasing airmindedness, the RAF, though recommended to boys as a career by some schoolmasters and relatives, was something of an adventure into the unknown. "In fact, a lot of people still thought it was the Royal Flying Corps, even in the 1930s."[14]

For 1931, the RAF was cutting its apprentice intake because of the government budget cuts. That August, the country slid into political crisis because of the worsening economic situation. Ramsay MacDonald was made prime minister of a new coalition government. He announced that his aim was to tackle the country's unemployment, "a menacing disgrace in our midst".

Meanwhile, the level of education in the general population was a continuing concern to educationists and others. The great majority of children, 90 per cent, left school at 14 – the national school-leaving age having been raised from 12 in 1918.

In 1922 the Labour party, in a report edited by the historian and socialist R H Tawney, called for secondary education for all children to age 16. Four years later, the Hadow Report recommended that schooling should be compulsory until age 15, pointing out the "grave waste… when education ceases abruptly at fourteen".

Proposals to raise the leaving age met resistance from influential people, educated at fee-paying schools and university. They believed the working classes had enough privileges. At the same time, many working-class parents did not want their children to remain at school beyond age 14, believing they should be at work earning to support the family.

Scholarships and free places only partly filled the gap in the availability of secondary schooling. Meanwhile, the stand-off over the leaving age continued. In the House of Lords in November 1930, during a debate on the Education (School Attendance) Bill, Sir Charles Trevelyan, President of the Board of Education, declared:

I want… to try to make the House fully realise how formidable and sweeping a change in education is in progress… No upper-class father fails to keep his son at school until 17 or 18, whether he be clever or stupid. And what has

been practised by the upper class for 200 years, it is time we began for the workers...
I refuse, until I see it, to believe that the Conservative party, even under the ingenious leadership of the Noble Lord [Lord Eustace Percy], is going all out against the raising of the school age to 15.[15]

The Bill, which was strongly backed by the Workers' Educational Association, did not go through. The third attempt failed in February 1931. It was rejected with "a levity and callousness which aroused the deepest resentment", according to Jimmy Mallon, an economist and political activist.

So while the majority of children still left school at 14 it was a future Ernest Deverill was fortunate to avoid, thanks to Chivers and his ambitious parents. Further general education in the RAF while he trained as an apprentice would put him, after three years, among the minority in the country schooled to Higher Education level.

This was a preparation for an uncertain world. And, as the Air Ministry promised, there was the opportunity to learn to fly.

UNDER ORDERS

The special train from London drew into Wendover station in the afternoon of Tuesday September 1 1931. As it eased to a halt the carriage doors swung open and nearly 400 boys spilled on to the platform gripping their suitcases. An RAF warrant officer on the platform took charge with his corporals and directed the crowd into the station yard. There the boys clambered into the back of three-ton lorries, which set off in convoy through the town.

A two-mile climb up a road between beech trees brought the vehicles to RAF Halton where they were driven on to the parade ground. Senior apprentices stepped forward and dropped the tailboards urging everyone to jump out, among them the dark-haired boy from Portsmouth, Ernest Deverill.

The large party was split up into groups of 20 "and led to a nearby dining hall where we were served with big plates of sausage and mash and mugs of hot strong tea". After the meal they were escorted to two-storey barrack blocks with rooms having 20 beds. Each boy was allocated a bed and helped to settle in. The RAF wasted no time. "We were warned that the next day would be a busy one and that, following the medical, we would be told whether or not we had been properly accepted into the service."[16]

In the morning, after breakfast, the new arrivals were taken to the medical in groups, wearing just a blanket in the room to provide a little modesty. The medical officers' inspection was rigorous – each boy "poked, prodded, weighed and measured, all the time being asked question

44

after question" – to confirm their general health and reject anybody with a condition that made him unfit for RAF service. Eyesight and hearing were carefully checked. A number of boys were rejected. They were driven back to the station with a rail warrant and sent home.

The successful majority were Halton's 24th apprentice entry. They were given vaccinations and queued at the barber's shop for the "inescapable short back and sides", taking less than two minutes per head.

The RAF was formed in the last year of WW1 by merging the Royal Flying Corps and Royal Naval Air Service. The Halton apprentice system was established in 1922 under a plan by Lord Trenchard, Chief of the Air Staff. Trenchard had recognised in 1919, in a government paper, that a peacetime RAF would have to train its own technical staff to maintain its aeroplanes and communications as there were few state technical schools.

By enlisting bright boys into its own scheme, he stated, the RAF could train them in three years instead of the five it took for a traditional apprenticeship.

"Boom" Trenchard, it was said, "had the stature, the heart and the voice of a giant" – "Boom" was his widely used nickname, even by friends, because of his gruff, barking voice. Those he worked with could not always understand what he was getting at, requiring his ideas to be "interpreted", yet Trenchard was far-sighted. His plan was that the boys' general education should continue alongside their technical training, to Higher School Certificate level, and he regarded the apprentice scheme as a way to foster "the Air Force spirit".

As an article in *Flight* magazine explained in 1923: "Thus the Air Force not only gets eventually an intelligent, efficient aircraftsman, but at the end of the latter's term of service in the RAF the country obtains a healthy, educated citizen capable of immediately following a skilled trade."[17]

Courses for engine and airframe apprentices were run at Halton. Those for electrical and wireless training – Instrument makers, Electricians, and Wireless operator/ Mechanics – were at the No.1 Electrical & Wireless School at RAF Cranwell, in Lincolnshire. Courses were held elsewhere for armourers. In the early 1930s the RAF's aeroplanes were little changed since WW1. Most were still open-cockpit biplanes made of wood, with fuselage and wings covered in doped fabric. The service continued to train apprentices in blacksmithing and fabric working.

The RAF experimented with monoplanes and all-metal planes but many in the service were sceptical about aeroplanes that did not have two wings braced with wires.

At Halton that first week each boy went before an interviewing board of senior officers who considered their aptitude, potential, and the trade they wished to enter. This was to guide the boys into a career that both met the RAF's manpower needs and offered good prospects.

The interviews were conducted in order of the exam results, so Ernest Deverill will have been among the first to be interviewed. His top marks for mathematics – 200 out of a possible total of 500 for the four papers – were what the RAF was looking for.

Ernest was accepted to train as a Wireless Operator/ Mechanic. This would qualify him to operate, maintain and repair the RAF's radio and electrical equipment both in the air and on the ground. As a Grade 1 trade, together with Instrument maker, Engine fitter, and Airframe rigger, Wireless Op/Mechanic was one of the most skilled and best paid, with excellent prospects of promotion. So his three-year apprenticeship would be at the wireless school.

Each new apprentice signed a Notice Paper that confirmed the 12 years of service they were committing to would start on their 18th birthday. In groups, they swore an oath on the Bible to serve the King. "Now that we had been sworn in, the flavour of events changed somewhat," one former entrant recalled. "Orders were now given, not requests, and the tiresome process of being changed from a... youth to the lowest form of life in the RAF was under way. We were each given a piece of paper with our service number written on it and told to memorise it."[18]

Next was the business of being kitted out. Typically this was a scramble:

During the issue of uniforms and kit we discovered that the RAF must have been comprised of gorillas and dwarfs, because of such difficulty in obtaining a proper fit... Finally, the overworked staff managed to locate enough uniforms to satisfy everyone and, draped with webbing, carrying armfuls of clothes and dragging kit bags, we set out looking like a mobile haberdasher's emporium.[19]

Now the boys had to parcel up the clothes they arrived in, with brown paper and string, and these were sent home – apprentices were not allowed to wear civilian clothing. On the left sleeve of their tunic they sewed a brass badge depicting a four-bladed propeller within a circle, and put a red band around their cap. This showed they were apprentices. Name tags had to be sewn on their new clothes, names marked or stamped on the rest of their kit, which included an aluminium mess tin and one-pint china mug with RAF crest, to drink the NAAFI tea.

The apprentice uniform was little changed from what British soldiers had worn in the 1914 war, or indeed British cavalrymen in the Boer War. It comprised a scratchy dog-collar tunic of thick blue serge, peaked cap, pantaloons (breeches) and puttees, with thick leather boots. A "voluminous" greatcoat was provided for cold weather, and apprentices had to carry a silver-tipped swagger cane for parades or while "walking out" from camp at weekends in "Best blue".

The uniform had been somehow cobbled together in this style under the influence of senior officers who had switched to a flying career from the Army. This was in an era when promotion prospects could be higher for a man who was "useful on a horse". Indeed, Trenchard himself led a mounted infantry unit during the Boer War.

One apprentice recalled that the standard-issue boots were "more like sheets of armour plate; toes and ankle bones were rubbed sore after the first few hours. The corporal in charge of our section told us to fill the boots with water, pee was best, and stand them by our beds overnight, empty them out and put them on straight away – they would never hurt again. He was right."[20]

Puttees were the most frustrating item of uniform to get used to. One ex-apprentice recalled that these "were cursed things which refused to conform to any known law". Another explains why:

They comprised two cloth strips one of which had to be wound carefully around each lower leg, overlapping and working upwards while providing the right amount of pressure to keep it in position.

The top spiral had to finish two fingers' width below the kneecap, and the end of the puttee

had to coincide with the seam of the breeches (a point for examination on parade inspections). Getting this wrong in haste could result in a swathe of material drooping round the ankles, and a charge for being improperly dressed.[21]

Thus kitted out, the new entry were marched from one part of the camp to another, shown round the workshops, and taught to march, and drill, on the parade ground until they were proficient. They were now subject to King's Regulations, the more than 1,300 pages of rules and detailed guidance on every aspect of Royal Air Force activity. This ranged from the flying, maintenance and inspection of aircraft, to the conduct of officers, the correct saluting of royalty, and weight of baggage the different ranks were allowed when posted abroad.

After two weeks at Halton, boys selected for the wireless school were ordered to pack their kit and marched to the station for a train to Grantham and on to Cranwell. Meanwhile, King's Regulations had not forgotten that its youngest recruits were growing lads. One clause stated that their greatcoats could be altered "at public expense" as a boy grew.

So, at $15\frac{1}{2}$, Ernest Deverill went into uniform and took the RAF number 565503. His pay would be 1 shilling a day for the next two years then 1s 6d ($7\frac{1}{2}$p) until he completed his training, in July 1934. As to where he might serve after qualifying, the Notice Paper he signed included the statement: "On enlistment into the Royal Air Force you will be liable, if medically fit, to carry out duty in the air in any type of aircraft and may be ordered to serve in any part of the world, ashore or afloat." With the British Empire ruling a quarter of the globe the RAF required nothing less than that.

IN TRENCHARD'S IMAGE

The No.1 Electrical & Wireless School occupied the East Camp at RAF Cranwell, in bleak open Lincolnshire countryside. Ernest Deverill arrived there, in uniform, with 70 other boys on September 16 1931. The camp had its own railway station, and extensive sidings, though the branch line was used mainly to bring in large quantities of heating coal. Sleaford, the nearest town, was five miles away.

Like the West Camp nearby, where RAF cadets trained to be officers, East Camp comprised a large collection of wartime buildings and huts put up in 1916 when the camp was opened as a Royal Naval Air Service station. Fifteen years later the buildings were showing their age.

Kay Carroll, a wing commander's wife who visited to attend functions, said her main impression of the East Camp was of "a vast conglomeration of corrugated iron. On a wet day the prospect is unspeakably depressing".[22]

The camp was dominated by the parade ground, the "sacred acre" apprentices were forbidden to step on except for drill and parades. The boys were housed in two-storey brick H-blocks, 40 to a room, each with an NCO (non-commissioned officer) in charge who had his own room.

Discipline in the Halton system is recalled by former apprentices as "firm but fair" – very strict to say the least. A good deal of time was spent doing drill exercises on the parade ground with little regard for the weather. Boys "very soon found their lives falling into a well-ordered routine governed largely by bugle calls".[23]

Reveille was sounded at 6.10am, Breakfast was at 6.45. Parade for workshops, and to hoist colours, was at 7.30, or for school at 7.50. The boys were marched about the camp to workshops and classrooms, and to the canteen carrying their "irons" – knife, fork and spoon. Dinner at 12:15pm was followed at 1.05 by Afternoon parade for workshops or school. Tea was at 5.00, Supper at 7.30, and Roll Call 8.45. Prayers were at 9.20 then Lights Out at 9.30. Church Service on Sunday mornings wearing "best blue" was compulsory, with few boys excepted.

Week-by-week records of the Electrical & Wireless School from that period have since been lost (some would say in a "bonfire" of archives in the 1960s). But the recollections of boys who trained there during the 1930s are vivid and typical of Ernest's experience.

Well recalled was the amount of "bull" enforced by the ex-Army NCOs, who had tight control of discipline. The night before Saturday morning barrack inspection everything had to be cleaned until it was spotless, as Michael Frere remembered:

Each barrack room contained a dustbin and two five-gallon tea buckets none of which were ever used for their designed purpose. Each had to be kept polished to eye-blinding brightness to satisfy inspecting officers.

The brown lino covering the floor also had to be polished to the point that no mark or smear spoiled the perfection of the surface. The same criteria applied to the brasswork of uniforms and webbing on display, and not a speck of dust was allowed to mar the surface of window sills or heating pipes.[24]

The technique for polishing the floor was that two boys applied the polish with cloth bumpers then several more skated slowly up and down in a swaying motion with pads under their feet to bring up the shine.

Iron bedsteads had the standard RAF mattress of three horsehair "biscuits" and hard horsehair pillow. For inspection, the biscuits had to be stacked square on the bed frame with blankets and sheets correctly wrapped round them, pillows on top. Personal kit in a metal locker above the bed had to be displayed with service number showing forward.

Any small mistake spotted, socks wrongly folded or shoes not perfectly clean, could bring a charge and several days' C.C. (confined to camp) with extra duties. There was no difficulty finding a punishment for minor offences. An ex-boy remembered that "moving the huge heaps of coal delivered by the railway to the back of the boiler house was one of the main fatigues for apprentices". After the inspection "the rest of Saturday was our own".

Michael Frere again:

Food was always good for a moan. Probably it wasn't too bad and probably sufficient, but as growing boys, and we all were, there was never enough!

Baked beans, scrambled eggs, boiled eggs (hard), sausages, bacon, liver, meat (we swore it was horse), potatoes, cabbage and suchlike were staple diet, along with bread and margarine, marmalade and jam. And sometimes, as a great treat, a stodgy piece of cake.[25]

The numbers of boys in close proximity, in barrack rooms and classrooms, was a constant concern to the medical staff. A morning "sick parade" was called by NCOs in the barrack rooms, and staff were ever watchful for serious infections such as diphtheria, or worse, meningitis, in case these spread through the camp. The procedure for any boy with symptoms was usually a spell of isolation in the camp hospital, the wards comprising a number of huts. Ernest Deverill was admitted several times during the three years.

It is almost certainly while he was at Cranwell that he began to smoke. Smoking was forbidden until the age of 18, when permits were issued to smoke in certain places, but to disregard this rule, out of sight of the NCOs, was a badge of honour. "The boy who didn't smoke was rather looked down on," one recalled.

Holiday leave totalled six weeks a year: three weeks in August, two at Christmas and one at Easter – enabling the apprentices to travel home to spend time with their family. There was also half-term leave. Parents were informed of the dates in advance "and boys will not be sent on leave until the approval of their parents or guardians has been received". Between times, since money was short, a Postal Order from home was gratefully received.

The working week for apprentices was 35 hours, made up of 18 hours in workshops; nine hours of physical training and organised games; and eight hours' schooling in maths, science, English subjects and drawing. The teaching, by civilian instructors, is recalled as being of a very high standard. One ex-apprentice wrote:

We were required to learn in great detail and often produce from memory the circuit diagrams of wireless transmitters, receivers, amplifiers and test equipment. We were also

taught to send and receive Morse Code at 25wpm [words per minute] and with flags or Aldis lamp at 12wpm and 8wpm respectively. Detailed theoretical and practical instruction was given on motors, generators, magnetos, petrol-electric charging sets, accumulators, aircraft and car wiring.[26]

There were no textbooks. Trainees in the Navy were using the specially written *Admiralty Guide to Wireless Telegraphy*, updated in 1931, but there was nothing like this yet at Cranwell. Boys had to take notes and draw diagrams during lectures, building up their own book with a record of what they learned. All those hours in the top room at Chivers will have stood Ernest in good stead.

To provide air experience, the wireless school had two aircraft and a transmitter station in the W/T block – called the "Taj Mahal". Here there were classrooms and an ageing T19 ground transmitter with a single "large glowing valve". Wireless telegraphy (W/T) was a general term for the field of radio communication.

The school's Vickers Victoria was a big 1920s biplane with twin engines and bulbous nose, designed originally as a troop carrier. Its pilot flew boys 12 at a time with their instructor, each boy sitting at a small desk with a radio set. At a suitable height they practised sending and receiving messages in Morse with the ground station as the aircraft rumbled sedately over the Lincolnshire countryside.

The second aircraft, a two-seat Armstrong Whitworth Atlas, was used to simulate service conditions, the pupil carrying out exercises from his drafty, uncomfortable position behind the pilot.

To improve their Morse speed the boys practised in their spare moments by tapping out messages and conversations on their tea mugs, or anything else handy to make a noise.

Rifle drill began in the second year, to sharpen parade ground discipline and ensure an immaculate performance, eventually, at the entry's passing out parade.

In their free time the boys visited the "Y" (YMCA),[27] the popular social centre in a large extended hut set away from the main area of the camp. With its range of social activities, and pastoral care, the Y offered a welcoming place to relax. Most boys had left home for the first time: some from a family short of money, others escaping a difficult home life. As an independent institution the Y was a respite from the wireless school's relentless discipline, part of the pledge to parents that the RAF would look after their sons.

Ewart Chorley, in his early thirties, took over as Secretary at the Y during Ernest's final year. He supported the boys, Chorley said, by offering "a home from home... a little friendly help, or a word of advice or counsel. It was the formative years for these youngsters and I did what I could to make their life in camp as pleasant as possible."[28] He paints a lively picture of the centre:

The main hall, which could seat about 400 and had a stage at one end, was used as the canteen, with the counter down one side. At the back of the hall, partitioned off, was a billiard and snooker room, (with two tables) and beyond this were two rooms for games, meetings etc. To brighten everything up there were huge paintings of aircraft of the first world war.

With the numbers of lads using the Y at morning and lunchtime breaks, the canteen was always more than a little hectic. Break times meant

**four continual queues until the bell went, three
girls pouring 'char' and serving 'wads', while
two more of the staff were weighing out 2oz
of a large variety of loose sweets and bars of
chocolate.**

**The favourite cake was the Nelson Cake, a slab
of bread pudding ¾in thick by 3in square with
slabs of pastry top and bottom. This together
with a mug of tea cost twopence.**

**'What's on at the Y' was a nightly cry in many
barrack rooms in the evenings, for there was
always something on. Table tennis, billiards,
snooker, chess tournaments and whist drives,
with suppers or cigarettes (if you had a smoking
pass) for prizes. These were always well
attended. Film shows were popular with silent
films shown to packed audiences.**[29]

Dancing was always a popular event, Ewart Chorley
recalled. "As ladies were not allowed on the camp, the boys
danced with each other to the music of their own excellent
dance band. A surprising number of boys learned to dance
in the Y at Cranwell, making them well able to 'strut their
stuff' in dance halls all over the country."

Other activities in the camp included ample sport on
Wednesday afternoons, model aeroplane club, several
bands, and a debating society. The energies and minds
of the apprentices were kept fully occupied at Cranwell.
While there was fun, pranks and high spirits, they were
left little time for their own thoughts, one ex-apprentice
remembered.

Lord Trenchard had officially retired from the Air
Force in 1929 but in reality only on paper; his continuing
activities behind the scenes as "father of the RAF"

remained a guiding presence. An observer of his influence was TE Lawrence, "Lawrence of Arabia", the man of action who led the Arab revolt against Turkish Ottoman forces during the 1914-18 War.

In the mid-1920s he had pulled strings in high places, appealing to his friend Boom, to help him enlist in the RAF in attempts to lead a life out of the public eye. So Lawrence was to be found working as a runner and clerk in a hanger at the cadet college at Cranwell. Granted his wish for anonymity as "Aircraftman Shaw" he held the lowly rank of AC2.

Lawrence rode an expensive 100mph Brough Superior motorcycle, admired on the West Camp, but he had the common touch unusual for somebody of his class. In his hut, he saw beyond his fellow rankers' grumbling, crude language and "silly laughter".

Describing their respect for the service, and Boom himself, he wrote: "Trenchard has designed the image he thinks most fitted to be an airman; and we submit our nature to his will, trustingly... The word Trenchard spells out confidence in the RAF and we would not lose it by hearing him decried. We think of him as immense… just by what he is."[30]

Lawrence was impressed by the Cranwell apprentices, who visited the West Camp for sports fixtures against the cadets, such as boxing. To Trenchard he wrote in 1928 "there is rising up a second category of airman, the Boy Apprentice... Soon the ex-Boy will be the majority, and the RAF I knew will be superseded and forgotten".[31] In turn, the apprentices in the Halton system had no doubts about their self-worth. They had a song that went:

Boom Trenchard loves us!
Boom Trenchard loves us!
Boom Trenchard loves us!
And so he bloody well should!![32]

Holiday leave from East Camp was a break from the discipline and work, also the relentless cleaning. Yet at each visit home the ordinary world must have seemed more distant to these boys. Their appearance and confident manner showed they were growing up fast as independent young men. Kay Carroll wrote:

> **Every time I attended a Wireless School function I was struck afresh by the amazingly high standard of looks and physique, their cheerful, carefree bearing, and their happy, frank outlook.**

> **There can be few careers more attractive than the RAF to the boy with brains who would otherwise find employment in a wireless shop or garage. The life is interesting and agreeable, with plenty of opportunities of travel; the pay for a trained man good.**[33]

In summer 1934, Ernest took his final trade exams with the rest of the 24th Entry. Of the 57 apprentices who trained as Wireless Operator/Mechanics, four passed as LAC (Leading Aircraftman), 27 passed as AC1 (Airman First Class) and 24 as AC2 (Airman Second Class), while two failed and were remustered.

Ernest finished among the AC1s, for which the marks required were 60-80 per cent and a Morse speed of at least 22 words per minute. He had earned his "sparks" wireless operator's badge, a hand grasping six lightning flashes, to sew on his tunic sleeve. His basic pay would be £77 a year; a Leading Aircraftman earned £100.

The commandant's final report on the 24th Entry praised the standard of games and athletics, and the boys' sports successes. They also had "done well in educational subjects". But the powers that be were not pleased by their general discipline, which had been "below normal". Cadetships were awarded to three of the apprentices passing out at Halton but, exceptionally, none was awarded at Cranwell. Those keen to become pilots would have to apply as LACs after a period of service.

Completion of the course was marked on Wednesday July 25 by the official inspection and passing-out parade, watched proudly by the boys' families. The inspecting officer was Air Vice-Marshal Wilfrid Freeman, Commandant of the RAF Staff College and a rising star in the service. Following established procedure he walked the lines of those leaving, and the younger apprentices, with his inspection party.

The march-past to stirring band music, with fixed bayonets and "a hint of swagger", carried the emotion of three years of hard work and achievement. For parents, officers, apprentices, it was a powerful display that these young men of 18, moulded to Trenchard's vision, had come of age, ready to serve their country.

Trained aircraftmen were required to serve abroad for a minimum of two years, with India, Egypt or Iraq the common postings. Egypt with its good climate and fascinating capital, Cairo, on the River Nile, was perhaps the most attractive posting. Colonial India was also an intriguing part of the world. However Iraq, with fierce summer heat, desert and dust storms, was a less agreeable prospect.

Ernest Deverill was listed for armoured car duties in Iraq, which required some special training in England before being sent out. This likely involved being taught to drive, and further training in gunnery. Meanwhile he was posted to RAF Gosport, a station crowded with various types of aircraft – close to Portsmouth and home via the Gosport ferry.

During this period, in spring 1935, he was attached for two months to the RAF School of Naval Co-operation at Lee-on-the-Solent, a short distance from Gosport. "The place was a hybrid affair in every way with a mixture of Royal Air Force and Royal Navy personnel", under the command of an RAF Group Captain.[34] Since Ernest was a wireless operator, the attachment was possibly for a signals course to learn current procedures for communicating with Navy vessels.

Considerable building work was being carried out at the aerodrome, a former seaplane base, to provide more accommodation under the RAF's new Expansion scheme. Yet the most prominent feature in the area was not the RAF station but Lee Tower, a strikingly modern leisure pavilion under construction on the seafront. When completed this Y-shaped building, gleaming white, would have a ballroom, roof terrace, Palm Court Café, and cinema. A viewing platform at the height of 120 feet would "provide an unrivalled sea view of the Solent and Isle of Wight".

It was not the only striking new building for leisure in the area. On the opposite side of Portsmouth Harbour the city council, joining a national trend for outdoor fitness, had opened Hilsea Lido, an impressive outdoor pool with a 10-metre diving tower, café, and open air dance floor for summer evenings, built in the new modern style. Ernest's sister Doreen, at 14, was one of the top junior swimmers at the opening event, in July 1935.

The Gosport posting probably was in part a wait before AC1 Deverill could travel to Iraq. Troopships for the Middle East sailed in winter to give new arrivals time to acclimatise ahead of the sweltering summer season. Temperatures in Iraq in August could reach 120degF in the shade.

Left: Ernest, aged two, with his mother Elsie and baby brother Derek, pictured at Chislehurst, 1918

Below left: Ernest Deverill snr, in Royal Navy uniform, pictured in 1919 with three of his four brothers (l to r) Frederick, Leonard and Frank, after their return from Army war service. Edgar was still abroad in Egypt

Below: Ship's postcard of the *Tamaroa*, the Shaw Savill Line steamer in which the Deverill family returned to England from New Zealand during 1928

Above: Sailors among strollers on the promenade at Southsea in the 1930s. Families in Portsmouth had the seaside on their doorstep and could take steamer trips along the coast

Below: Chivers, the school where Ernest Deverill crammed for his apprentice exams, looms (centre) at the end of Somers Road on a wet day in 1932. At lunchtime boys crossed the street to buy liquorice sticks and ice-creams

Left: Flying Officer Henry Waghorn climbs into his Supermarine S6, engine running, at Calshot before winning the 1929 Schneider Trophy race at 328.63mph

Below: Crowds pack Southsea seafront on race day to watch the Schneider contest, an international event which gripped 'airminded' Britain that summer

Royal Aeronautical Society/Mary Evans Picture Library

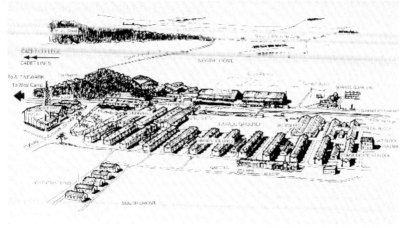

The East Camp at RAF Cranwell in 1936. The parade ground, centre, dominates the site. Far left is the YMCA, the popular social centre that offered apprentices respite from the strict discipline

ELECTRICAL INSTRUCTION

Left: Boys in class at the wireless school in the 1930s, an experience familiar to Ernest Deverill. From a cigarette card set titled Life in the Services

Left: 'Boom' Trenchard, 'father of the RAF', inspects aircraft apprentices at their passing out parade, RAF Halton about 1928. The apprentices are wearing the 'cursed puttees'

Studio portrait of Sgt Ernest Deverill in 1939-40 about the time he became engaged to Joyce. Above the sergeant's stripes on his sleeve is his 'sparks' wireless operator's badge

Crews of RAF No.1 Armoured Car Company, in which Ernest Deverill served as a wireless operator, take a rest break in the desert of Mesopotamia

RAF Habbaniya Association

Above: Joyce, at right, and Rita Burgis — sisters with very
different temperaments

Below: 'Dev' and Joyce, left, relax outside the farmhouse at Docking with
family and friends. Richard Burgis is fourth from left, Blanche at far right,
and John, Joyce's brother, next to Blanche

Above: Docking between the wars. Roy's was the village department store, selling groceries, household goods and drapery

Below: Lockheed Hudsons of Coastal Command on the apron at RAF Ringway, where Ernest Deverill was sent on a 10-day course to convert to the new aircraft

Left: Bombing up a
206 Squadron Hudson
at RAF Bircham
Newton, early June
1940, when
England faced the
peril of invasion

Below: Hudsons on
patrol over the North
Sea. The squadron
log shows that Sgt
Deverill is flying in
C-Charlie (P5120)
as second pilot

DESERT AND MARSH

The three-week voyage from Southampton to Iraq on the troopship *Dorsetshire* was no pleasure cruise. AC1 Deverill was one of hundreds of men packed below decks in conditions that were "pretty rough", and packed on deck during the day. The vessel, a modest 450 feet in length, had been converted from a cargo ship to accommodate 112 families in First class, 58 in Second and 108 families in Third, plus 1,450 Army men.

"Troopships were smelly, cramped, we slept in hammocks, they were anything but pleasant," recalled another aircraftman on board the ship.[35]

Dorsetshire left England in the last week of January 1936 and steamed through the Suez Canal and Red Sea. She arrived at Basrah at the head of the Persian Gulf, where the RAF men transferred directly to the railway station. Here they crowded into a train of "tin trucks" for the 230-mile overnight journey to Baghdad. Officers, meanwhile, travelled in some comfort on the night sleeper.

Ernest Deverill's posting was to the No.1 Armoured Car Company based at RAF Hinaidi, the RAF's main command and technical base in Iraq. Situated seven miles from Baghdad beside the River Tigris, it was a huge camp encircled by a bund, the big embankment protecting it from floods during the winter rains. The old but often-used name for Iraq was Mesopotamia, the ancient region "between two rivers", the Tigris and Euphrates.

The RAF's presence in Mesopotamia – "Mespot" to old hands in the service – came about in the aftermath of

WW1. The League of Nations had given Britain a mandate to administer Iraq, Palestine and the state of Transjordan.

In London, however, the government could not justify the enormous costs required to maintain peacetime garrisons of thousands of troops in Iraq to police the country and quell tribal unrest. Lord Trenchard, facing the risk that the RAF would be disbanded, had a plan. He lobbied Winston Churchill, Secretary of State for Air, proposing that deploying eight squadrons of aircraft and a number of RAF armoured car companies in the region would be an effective, much cheaper solution.

His enthusiasm perhaps running away with him, Trenchard also floated the idea, in 1920, that in the event of violent disturbances in British cities the government could adopt similar methods and sanction "a limited amount of [RAF] bombing and machine-gun fire".[36] Churchill quickly scotched this possibility before it could find its way into official policy.

By 1936, when Ernest Deverill arrived at Hinaidi, the RAF was policing Iraq under a treaty, with two British Army battalions in barracks in Transjordan 500 miles to the west. Serious disturbances in Transjordan in 1929 showed that, in practice, armoured cars and aircraft had to be reinforced by troops. Neat lines of administration had been drawn on a Middle East map by the Western powers yet the region, under Turkish rule for 500 years until WW1, was inhabited by many different tribes, ethnic and religious groups. There were Arabs in towns, nomadic Bedouin in the desert, Kurdish tribes in the mountains, marsh Arabs in the south.

Old alliances and feuds continued among the tribes, who were commonly armed with rifles. In Transjordan were disputes and worse between Arabs and incoming

Jewish immigrants who had left Europe to escape the worsening situation in Nazi Germany.

RAF rankers, as new arrivals from Britain, were greeted in typical service fashion. Frank Canvin, a gunner in No.1 Armoured Car Company, recalled: "Having had our pure white knobbly knees admired and the sartorial elegance of our issue khaki drill ridiculed, we paraded before the flight sergeant of the section. He handed us down to the sergeant, and so down to the corporals, each of whom were car commanders.

"Having made it plain that, this time, the Air Ministry had definitely scraped the bottom of the barrel, we were allocated to vehicles."[37]

There was a certain respect for the efficient young men sent out after being trained in the Halton system. Across the RAF they earned the name "Trenchard's Brats". However, AC1 Deverill's new duties were interrupted only a week after he arrived at Hinaidi. He was put in the camp hospital for seven days, perhaps because of an infection caught on the ship or soon after. The English nurses who staffed the hospital were the only women on the camp.

No.1 Armoured Car Company comprised four sections. Deverill was put into Section 2 or Section 3 and may have served in both – records from that time are scarce and mostly only officers were mentioned by name. From Hinaidi, the cars of these two sections were sent on patrols through swamps, mountains and into the desert.

A patrol comprised a Rolls-Royce armoured car, a wireless tender, plus Albion and Crossley lorries to carry kit that included vehicle spares, food, cooking and camping equipment. A fighting section comprised four armoured cars, wireless tender and two armed lorries. A larger force of perhaps 30 vehicles could be assembled for action if required – "control without occupation" as the British called it.

The armoured cars carried a crew of three cramped in the confined space: commander, driver and gunner. The main armament was a Vickers machine gun in a large rotating turret, with a searchlight for night operations.

Signal flags were stored in clips on the turret roof ready for use, enabling car commanders to communicate visually with other cars. The Rolls-Royce vehicles were robust but spartan bare metal inside, a seat cushion for the driver the only comfort. His view ahead was through a narrow slot.

Patrols were carried out in conditions that "were hostile, temperatures ranging well above 100degF in the day during the summer to freezing cold at night. The terrain varied from arid desert of sand, rock and stones, to mountains, to salt marsh in which vehicles sank up to their axles. The cars were manhandled on to local ferries and even makeshift rafts to transport them across rivers."[38]

Patrol routes in "the blue", the vast stony desert between Baghdad and Transjordan, were along faint tracks. In late spring and summer huge choking sand storms turned the skies orange.

These were conditions unchanged since Lawrence of Arabia's exploits in 1917, when he led the Arab revolt against forces of the Turkish Ottoman Empire. "With non-existent roads, countless wadis to cross, quagmires to be dug out of when it rained and sharp stones lacerating tyres, the crews had to be self-sufficient. They were almost totally reliant on their practical skills and initiative."[39]

Frank Canvin wrote: "Some of these routine trips could last up to five weeks from the base station and the mobility of the section was of prime importance. Nothing of a personal nature was carried on the cars and all bedrolls and kit were stowed on the Albion. Tents, a breadbox, food supplies and any heavy stores were loaded on the Crossley.

"The routine task was the marking and inspection of the tracks that served for roads, also assisting with vehicle breakdowns and at aircraft crashes, and 'showing the flag' at intervals in major towns."

A meal stop in the desert invited the perpetual nuisance of sandflies, while sand and dust found its way into the food. Water was carried in pannier tanks but its use closely watched, hence an official instruction: "Cooking utensils and plates can be cleaned in dry sand and finally polished with paper". Strict use of water meant that personal hygiene on patrols was "very sketchy", Canvin recalled.

The desert was thinly populated by nomadic Bedouin who camped in black goats-hair tents, their camels and sheep nearby. RAF policing since the early 1920s included intervening in disputes over access to water holes, theft of camels, and controlling rebellious tribes. In Britain, the RAF's willingness to bomb villages in Iraq, to force compliance, aroused serious disquiet.

A firsthand account of a policing sortie in Iraq appeared in 1931 in *The Modern Boy's Book of Aircraft*, under the title Wings of the Desert. A flying officer "who prefers his name not to be known" described a "thrilling adventure" in 1926.

Three aircraft were sent to intercept raiders who had stolen "a big bunch of camels, horses and sheep", he wrote. Spotting them, "Our flight leader pushed his stick forward and down we went, our forward Vickers guns chattering and our observers bringing their Lewis guns to bear as we flattened out.

"Three such dives and several saddles were emptied,

the riderless horses and camels following the main body... Our mission was now accomplished for the time being, as far as we were concerned. It would take the armoured cars to round up the cattle and bring in any wounded men."

Ernest Deverill's duties in the wireless tender will have kept him well occupied as communications with other cars, and with aircraft, had to be maintained by various means: messages in Morse, lamp signals, and "that very useful method – semaphore". This set his work apart to some extent. "Not being a fighting vehicle, and having a wireless operator as part of the crew, the spirit aboard was far more relaxed than that on an armoured car," Canvin said.

The cook "would put up a scratch midday meal as camp was only formed at night. The one exception being the crew of the wireless tenders. As they often had a signal watch after we had broken camp and moved on, they carried their own kit on these vehicles.

"With only the wireless equipment, these tenders were much lighter than the cars and therefore travelled faster," Canvin recalled. However, they had a Lewis gun for defence, and each man on a patrol was armed with a rifle and Webley pistol.

Even forming camp was brought to a fine art. This required vehicles in correct position, gunpit on the corner, turrets swung, gun covers off, kitchen site and firepit dug, wireless mast erected and earth mat buried, auxiliary vehicles unloaded and tents erected.

When on the outskirts of a town during a 'showing the flag' recce, we even went to the extent of a flag mast flying the RAF ensign.

At Hinaidi, the working day for armoured car

personnel was leisurely by contrast. It mainly comprised maintaining the vehicles, by the mechanics, practising repairs for breakdowns likely to occur on patrol, plus practice on the firing range. In summer, most of this work was carried out early in the morning and in the evening because of the high temperatures in the middle of the day.

Meanwhile, the camp had ample off-duty activities to keep its airmen occupied: sports grounds, education classes, a cinema and big open-air swimming pool. In Baghdad, "a maze of narrow alleyways", the market with merchants selling carpets, old guns and copper bowls was intriguing and "something to see". Parts of the city were out of bounds to keep the men away from the brothels.

There were opportunities to visit the ancient ruins of Mesopotamia. The mud-brick remains of Babylon, south of Baghdad and dating back to 2,300BC, were sited by the River Euphrates. At Mosul in the north, remains of the Assyrian city of Nineveh occupied the east bank of the Tigris.

Only 15 miles from Hinaidi stood the Arch of Ctesiphon, a vaulted structure 100 feet high said to be the throne room remaining from a royal palace.

Such sites had been familiar to travellers and writers such as TE Lawrence and Gertrude Bell, Arabic speakers who closely identified with Arab culture. Bell, who advised the British administration in the 1920s, and herself an accomplished archaeologist, had been welcomed for coffee in the tents of desert sheikhs.

In 1936, however, all was not quite as timeless as it appeared. Bell had written, 20 years earlier: "The amazing quickness of the Arab in adopting himself to new conditions and profiting by unexpected opportunities must never be forgotten. A child born yesterday in a reed hut or a goats-hair tent may well be found practising medicine or the law in Baghdad before the next quarter of a century is over."

Everyday life in Iraq was seen in more humdrum terms by RAF airmen. An engine fitter working on armoured cars at Hinaidi recalled: "You always had the feeling that if you were British you were bloody good and the rest of the world, well, they were definitely second-class citizens. That was the attitude we had instilled into us. At the same time, there was a feeling of respect between one and the other."[40]

This idea of superiority was reinforced when the patrols met tribal opposition. The RAF's *Armoured Car Manual* stated:

> **Vigorous offensive action, combined with due precautions against ambushes and unexpected moves on the part of the enemy, should always be employed.**
> **The fire power of armoured cars is always superior to native forces, and cars must be so disposed that the maximum fire power is available at any given point.**
> **The morale of tribesmen is easily shaken, and as soon as their cohesion has been broken a relentless pursuit must be undertaken in order to prevent them reforming.[41]**

In spring 1936, not long after Ernest Deverill arrived at RAF Hinaidi, civil unrest flared up again in Palestine, beginning to repeat the events of 1929. There were riots at Jaffa in mid-April, protesting at the increasing numbers of Jewish refugees arriving to escape fascism in Europe. And demands for Arab economic independence, leading to a countrywide strike being declared by the Arab National Committee.

On May 8, as the situation worsened, the British forces declared an Emergency. At Hinaidi the two armoured car sections were ordered "to stand by to proceed at very short notice to Palestine to act as reinforcements", to the British Army units there. Next day, 2 and 3 Sections drove out of the camp to make the difficult journey to the other side of the desert. They reached Amman, east of the River Jordan, "in 40 hours' running time".

No.2 section was sent to RAF Ramleh east of Jerusalem, No.3 to Talevera Barracks in Jerusalem where the Cameron Highlanders were garrisoned. Though it is not known which section Deverill served in at this time, both saw action amid the unrest in the following weeks.

Each section was split into half-sections to carry out particular tasks. These included patrols, escorting senior personnel and the Camerons' lorries, and maintaining a wireless watch when required. On June 11, half of 3 Section on a night patrol with Cameron Highlanders in two lorries encountered a barricade of stones on the road, coming under fire for 30 minutes with "four Camerons injured". Some days later, the two sections drove back across the desert to Hinaidi. Meanwhile the unrest continued: by July the British were facing guerrilla warfare.

On July 1, Ernest was promoted to Leading Aircraftman, which suggests he performed his duties well in Palestine. Significantly, this promotion put him in a good position to apply for flying training. And fortunately the RAF, as part of its Expansion programme, was looking actively to train men from the ranks as sergeant pilots. Under the Expansion scheme, elementary training was being provided at newly set up civilian flying schools in England.

Back in Britain, the armed services were preparing for

the possibility of a war in Europe. In 1937, Ernest's father was recalled from his retirement by the Royal Navy to serve again, under a general order to bring back men over 50.

As well as increasing the Navy's strength, this would bolster the Navy with the experience of those "who had seen it all" in WW1. For Ernest senior, the call took him back to sea to use his technical knowledge. He was posted to join the 550 crew on the light cruiser *Ajax*. By February 1938 *Ajax* was on station in the West Indies.

LAC Deverill returned to England by troopship in early 1938 and was sent on leave. In a family photograph the Deverills are sitting on the beach, most likely at Southsea. Ernest is at the front of the group, his deep tan with brown knees could only be from his recent service in Mespot.

INTO THE SKIES

Leading Aircraftman Deverill reported to RAF Uxbridge, on the western outskirts of London. Uxbridge was the RAF's central administrative depot, where TE Lawrence had enlisted in the RAF ranks as "Aircraftman Shaw". Ernest Deverill was attached here for several weeks, with others also joining the same elementary flying course. They were kitted out with flying clothes and sent on leave while waiting for it to start.

On April 4 1938 he reported to No.2 Elementary & Reserve Flying Training School at RAF Filton, Bristol. The flight instructors at 2 ERFTS were RAF Reserve officers and wore civilian clothes, as did the pupils for the two-month course.

The school's aircraft was the de Havilland D82 Tiger Moth, with two open cockpits, the RAF's standard elementary trainer. Again Deverill was fortunate. In 1938 the RAF began teaching to a new standard training programme with the flying, backed by ground teaching, comprising a series of 25 graded exercises. His instructor was Flt Lt Younghusband.

Flying lessons began with "Familiarisation with controls", followed by successive exercises under the overall watch of the chief flying instructor (CFI) – take-offs, turns, "circuits and bumps" to practice landings. This was to build up a pupil's competence to make his first solo flight.

Not obvious from the syllabus, while managing

the manoeuvres and proper use of the aircraft's basic instruments, was learning the instinctive aspects of piloting an aircraft. The flow of air itself provided feedback to the pupil: the rush of the slipstream, changes in lift under the wings, were inputs to the senses – literally "seat of the pants flying".

Flt Lt D'Arcy Greig, who came third in the 1929 Schneider Trophy race, also was a staff instructor at the Central Flying School. He wrote: "An instructor must study the psychology of his pupil to ascertain the best line of approach to his mentality... An instructor must be patient with the backward pupil and quick to correct the overconfident one."

Filton's instructors used textbook patter (standard phrases) to teach the exercises, repeating them as required to progress each pupil and help them overcome weak points in their flying. Poor or unsafe landings were the common block to achieving the first solo.

A good landing required a well-judged approach, flattening out above the grass with a steady pull back on the stick, to lose speed and stall the airflow over the wings. Correctly done, this put the aircraft down in a "three-pointer" on its wheels and tail skid. It required repeated 'circuits and bumps' with the instructor until an acceptable standard was reached. Several pupils who could not assess their landing height properly were "sent away".

Seven or eight hours' dual instruction often were sufficient to go solo, while "a natural pilot" might do it in four or five. But ten hours reached with no solo raised questions about a pupil's suitability to fly in the RAF. Sometimes a "progress report" and change of instructor made the difference.

Deverill flew his first solo on April 11 in Tiger Moth

G-ACBG, making two circuits and landings, after 9 hours 20 minutes' dual instruction. Then the exercises progressed: more circuits and moving on to steep turns, stall turns, side-slipping, low flying; and aerobatics – slow rolls, loops, and spinning.

Aerobatics were taught to show pupils their capability to control an aircraft and learn its limitations. Instructors looked for clean, confident, accurate flying. In short, mastery of the machine.

The ground training meanwhile included learning Morse code and signalling with an Aldis lamp. While some on the course struggled to learn Morse and reach ten or 12 words per minute, Deverill's 20-plus from his apprentice days and Mespot service was ample. Near the end of the course came written exams which included papers on airmanship and basic navigation. Then the CFI went up with each pupil to make his final assessment.

Ernest Deverill was assessed on June 8 and his flying log book duly stamped to state he had completed the course successfully. He had flown 27 hours of dual instruction and 23½ hours solo. The course allowed 25 hours for each.

The CFI wrote in his rating of this new pilot's ability. In the RAF, a pilot's logbook was endorsed regularly during his flying career using the standard wording: "Below Average", "Average", "Above average". Or, more rarely, "Exceptional". Deverill was rated Average, indicating solid competence.

There was space on the page to record "Any special faults in flying which must be watched". This was left reassuringly blank. Next came the advanced course to learn to fly twin-engine aircraft to full service standards. For this Ernest Deverill was posted to the north of England.

MARGINS FOR ERROR

RAF Sealand was a huge, sprawling site near Chester that comprised two aerodromes divided by a railway line. Its main activity was dismantling and packing aeroplanes for shipment to stations overseas. It was also the home of No.5 Flight Training School, to which Ernest Deverill was posted in mid-June 1938 for a six-month course. He had about 90 hours of flying ahead of him to earn his pilot's wings and be made a sergeant pilot.

Again his timing was fortunate. The training aircraft at Sealand was the new Airspeed Oxford, a substantial twin-engine monoplane with advanced features for its time. Its capabilities enabled pilots, navigators and gunners to transfer without fuss to the more complex fighters and bombers coming into service.

"The Oxford was spirited, knew how to drop a wing at the stall and could swing quite energetically on landing, so it was a good pilot trainer," one pilot recalled. A drawback for the course was the Oxford had flown for the first time only the previous year. As a result, the instructors' experience on the machine was four hours or less. This intake of trainees were "guinea pigs" since their instructors were still working out the teaching techniques.

A key advance in the cockpit was the standard blind-flying panel, adopted by the RAF two years earlier. The six instruments essential to fly in cloud or at night in a modern aeroplane were logically grouped in two rows facing the pilot: air-speed indicator, artificial horizon and rate-of-climb indicator in the top row; altimeter, direction indicator and turn-and-bank indicator beneath. This innovation was well overdue because aircraft designers continued to mount instruments and controls in the cockpit at random, potentially confusing pilots at a critical moment.

This was demonstrated on the Oxford by the placing of the undercarriage and flap levers. These were "side by side on the central binnacle and almost indistinguishable from each other", an instructor recalled.

If a pupil selected flaps instead of pulling the undercarriage lever "the aircraft would sink like a free-falling lift and strike the ground with disastrous results... Like other instructors, I was living on my nerves when pupils were being taught to land, take off, and stall in the air. There was no margin for error."[42]

Deverill was one of 11 regular airmen on the course training to be sergeant pilots. Making up the total of 37 were 26 men who had enlisted recently from civilian life on a short-service commission. They would be made pilot officers. The 11 quickly found that while all the group were taught from the same syllabus, by the same instructors, the recent recruits messed separately. They used the officers mess while the prospective sergeants had to use the mess for other ranks.

This smaller group, with years of RAF service behind them, compared their career prospects with those of the soon-to-be officers and were not happy. One of them, Maurice Stretton, who had moved up from the elementary course with Deverill, said:

Our attitude was we'd had a rough deal. We all were well-educated ex-grammar school boys who had come into the Air Force when the depression was on – there were just no jobs at all.

We'd had to fight and struggle and had a tough existence in the ranks to attain what we had and, at the end of it, we'd still only be sergeants. Whereas these youngsters, just because of fate, had been able to step in, many of them with qualifications far less than ours. We felt it was an injustice but had to put up with it.[43]

So they referred to the recent recruits mockingly as "Sainsbury's boys – as if they were ex-grocers' assistants". Ernest Deverill could hardly have escaped the thought that this state of affairs reflected his father's progress in the Navy.

The advanced course was taught in three parts. The first was mastering the Oxford; the second, advanced flying, which included low flying, bad weather flights, and flying on one engine. This led to night flying on triangular cross-countries. One of these routes was Sealand to Bristol, a turn to Birmingham – "all the lights were on and you couldn't possibly miss" – and back to Sealand.

With more to think about at higher speeds, there were accidents from pupils' mistakes, and several funerals held during the course. For the third part, pupils flew to the north Wales coast in the first week of December for a month of military training at RAF Penrhos, on the Llyn peninsula. The exercises there comprised air gunnery, firing at a towed drogue, and bombing at the offshore range.

Deverill's logbook shows he returned to Sealand on January 6 with the course almost over and on the 12th was signed off. The CFI's rating was a bonus – "Above average". He had gained his "wings" as a sergeant pilot, a significant achievement given that his own "rough deal" had lasted seven years. The posting that followed was a signpost to his future career in the RAF.

Next, Ernest Deverill found himself in a select group when he reported to the School of General Reconnaissance, for a specialist navigation course, on January 14 1939. The four-month course was based at RAF Thorney Island, on the South Coast, not far from Portsmouth. This was for airmen with special aptitude as the RAF sought to catch up with an increasing need for accurate navigation to fly at night and over the sea.

For much of the 1930s the service officially had taken little interest in navigation beyond teaching the standard "dead reckoning" method. Dead reckoning (from deduced reckoning), involved the pilot calculating a course and entering it on a map.

A course-and-distance calculator was used to factor in wind direction, to set a compass course, since an aeroplane in the skies is carried with the wind. For this reason, dead reckoning has been described as "finding where the aircraft is being blown to and correcting its track to arrive at your destination". As yet there was no separate trade of navigator in the RAF.

In commercial aviation, advanced navigation techniques had to be applied to fly long long-distance routes over the oceans. By contrast, the training of RAF pilots was mostly concerned with flying skills. Like pleasure flyers, they flew mainly by day. To check where they were they relied on their flying maps, the aircraft compass, and on "Bradshawing" – after the railway timetable. That is, following a railway line whenever possible. However work was going on in the RAF to devise better navigation methods.

The course at Thorney taught the latest navigation and reconnaissance techniques. It had lecture rooms and an operations room and Sgt Deverill was one of 200 pilots taking the course that year. Thorney aerodrome was well situated for this advanced training since it was on land that stuck out into the Solent, the English Channel beyond.

The unit flew twin-engine Avro Ansons: "Noisy, smelly and not particularly comfortable", as one pilot remembered them. The Anson had gone into service as a four-seat charter plane for Imperial Airways in the mid-1930s, then was ordered in numbers by the Air Ministry for reconnaissance duties.

A rugged monoplane with wooden wings, it was "exceptionally docile" to fly, giving "a sense of reliability and confidence".[44] This, plus the large cockpit windows, made it an ideal aircraft for observation.

The air navigation exercises ranged along England's South Coast and as far as the Channel Islands. A staff pilot took students up in pairs. However, the second navigator was given an extra task. The Anson had no hydraulic system to raise and lower its undercarriage so it had to be done manually, after take-off and before landing. This required about 150 turns on a crank handle beside the pilot's seat and "five minutes of very hard puffing".

A new instrument used on the course was the bubble sextant, an adapted version of the traditional ship's sextant, to check an aircraft's position by "astronomical navigation". Fortunately, the RAF had adopted astro navigation as standard procedure for general reconnaissance, and for bomber pilots, less than 18 months earlier.

To become competent in "astro" required learning to recognise the fixed stars and their constellations by position in the night sky, and their appearance, such as bluish-white or reddish-yellow light. Among them were Polaris the Pole star, Orion, Cassiopeia, Perseus and Ursa Major. The sextant was used at night, by taking star shots through the astrodome in the Anson's roof.

Three shots were required to account for inaccuracies, then the navigator entered the corresponding positions on his chart by referring to a set of astronomical tables. The three positions formed a "cocked hat", with the aircraft assumed to be at the centre.

Cloudy skies or bumpy motion of the aircraft made operating the sextant an awkward task lasting perhaps 20 minutes. As a new navigation manual cautioned, the constellations were named in the distant past "according to very imaginative figures which they were supposed to represent... But it is recommended that the navigator should not strain his imagination by attempting to see these figures in the constellations".[45]

Also taught on the course were search techniques to locate a vessel, and skills to fly accurately to a position over the sea. Further, it was necessary to understand the behaviour of an aircraft compass under varying conditions, to be able to trust it.

This all gave the clue to a decisive next move: to bombers or Coastal Command. The course finished in the first week of May. When Ernest Deverill's posting came through his destination was a Coastal Command aerodrome on England's East Coast, on the other side of the country.

WAR ABOVE THE SEA

RAF Bircham Newton was situated in north Norfolk, surrounded by farmland, woods and a few scattered villages. Getting there involved changing trains at King's Lynn, then the village station at Heacham. From the branch-line platform, a few times a day, a humble locomotive hauled three old gas-lit coaches up the 18-mile single track to Wells-next-the-Sea.

Part way, the station at Docking was nearest to the aerodrome. Motor transport was sent from the camp to the station yard to collect arriving airmen. If transport was not available it was a three-mile walk. Sgt Deverill reported at the guardroom on May 6 1939 for service with 206 Squadron of Coastal Command, flying Avro Ansons. He was allocated accommodation in the sergeants' barracks.

Many RAF aerodromes were closed, and thousands of aeroplanes scrapped, when the RAF was run down after WW1. Bircham Newton remained open as a peacetime station because of its important maintenance workshops. Enlarged in 1936-37, Bircham had impressive buildings in the modern Georgian style adopted by the RAF under its Expansion plan. The almost-new offices, barracks and imposing brick hangars spoke of a leisured peacetime establishment.

This was clearly evident inside the well-appointed officers mess. Its high ceiling, fine proportions and comfortable furniture were designed to provide officers with a familiar setting "something between the country house and a large hotel".[46] Day by day this was a privileged world of waiter service, air force banter, and full-dress dining-in nights with "snowy white tablecloths and gleaming silverware".[47]

The RAF still drew many of its pilots from the educated classes who had luncheon and dressed for dinner. This lay behind the formalities between officers and other ranks, such as air gunners; and the ground crew earning flying pay to crank the Ansons' wheels up and down. In the air, little passed between pilot and crew beyond brief exchanges about the task in hand. "We didn't talk to pilots about the flying – they were all officers," as one ranker put it.[48]

RAF stations in the countryside were "virtually isolated from civilian life", a psychologist has pointed out. "The station was therefore a closed community, or rather two closed communities, one of officers and one of airmen, with the sergeant pilots occupying a slightly ambiguous position." Yet Trenchard's vision of an air force based on individual merit was coming true. The increasing numbers of apprentices rising in rank, also sergeant pilots such as Ernest Deverill, were testament to this.

By May 1939 the peacetime atmosphere at Bircham was evaporating like sea mist: 206 Squadron flying its Ansons was in readiness for war, its silver aircraft repainted in camouflage green and brown. Deverill was flying as second pilot with a number of Anson captains. He would be given first-pilot status after gaining experience.

The training took the Anson crews far into the North Sea using astro navigation as well as dead reckoning. Like others who had been through the School of General Reconnaissance, Deverill found the RAF was determined to use what he had learned to the full.

On the first day of September German forces invaded

Poland. Two days later, on September 3, the British government handed the German government in Berlin the "final note" seeking an undertaking that its troops would be withdrawn.

Sgt Deverill's war began that morning. He landed from a patrol at 11.15 am, when Neville Chamberlain, the Prime Minister, gave his fateful radio broadcast to the nation, stating:

"... I have to tell you now that no such undertaking has been received, and that consequently this country is at war with Germany".

It was also the day that Ernest Deverill was certified to fly the Anson as first pilot.

Waiting on the other side of the North Sea were Messerschmitt 109 single-seat fighters, formidably armed with 20mm cannon and machine guns. They had a speed advantage of more than 100mph over the Ansons. The Germans also had Heinkel He115 twin-engine floatplanes, a reconnaissance aircraft of businesslike appearance with three crew. The He115 was not much faster than the Anson but its two machine guns warranted respect.

However the Anson, though reliable, was far from ideal as a war machine. Its range of 600 miles did not leave a great deal of time to patrol off the Dutch and German coast 200 miles away. Also, it was lightly armed with only two .303 machine guns for defence.

Britain's declaration of war pitched Coastal Command and 206 Squadron into frontline defence of the country. The sorties comprised reconnaissance and anti-submarine patrols off the Dutch/German coast, protecting fishing vessels and escorting convoys on the East Coast.

One of the main duties was the dawn patrol, for which

a night take-off put the aircraft off the enemy coast at first light to observe any activity. The squadron motto was *Nihil nos effugit* – "Nothing escapes us".

Just two days after Britain declared war, came a shock at Bircham when an Anson failed to return. The crew had taken off at 5.30am to carry out a sea search with other aircraft near the Fresian Islands but became overdue. Nothing was heard from them.[50]

Protecting the East Coast convoys was a key task as the weeks passed. A convoy could total 40, 50 or more ships steaming south daily from the Firth of Forth and River Tyne with essential supplies for London, then back the following day in ballast. Many were colliers laden with coal from northern pits to keep the capital's factories going and the lights on.

These vessels sailing at six or seven knots, in a column five to ten miles long, were easy prey for German bombers and the fast, well-armed torpedo E-boats. Convoys followed a marked route between wrecks and natural dangers off the coast of East Anglia, "a maze of shoals and sandbanks", as a midshipman on an escort destroyer said. The E-boats also mined the navigation channel – the so-called "E-boat Alley". Masts of sunken ships pointing from the water were a constant reminder of the dangers.

These convoy patrols, also carried out by Blenheim bombers from Bircham Newton, and RAF fighters, were therefore a big responsibility. One Anson pilot recalled:

You were given an approximate, hoped-for position to meet a convoy… in hundreds of square miles of water. You had to plot your own track to go and meet it, and if you didn't meet it then you had to carry out a square search, or a line-ahead or line-astern search. You had to take decisions.[51]

Flying conditions could be difficult. At times the sea was an "oily calm", at others practically invisible in poor weather. "When the clouds were low and rain and sleet reduced the visibility to only hundreds of yards you had to balance the importance of the job against the fact that it was now getting dangerous to fly...

"You often ended up squeezed into a couple of hundred feet of airspace between the grey wispiness of the cloudbase and the heaving desolation of the North Sea below."[52]

A young Navy midshipman may have said it all in 1916 when he wrote in his diary: "The North Sea at its best is but a dull place, and as winter begins to come it is a most God-forsaken hole, with continuing rain, mist, fogs, alternating with gales and rough weather."[53]

Anson crews also had to cope with low cloud and sea mists rolling in to Bircham aerodrome from the sea, so that finding the circuit and landing after a patrol could be hazardous.

In December 1939, Ernest's father as a torpedo officer on *Ajax* played his part in the sinking of the heavy cruiser *Admiral Graf Spee* – the "Battle of the River Plate". *Ajax* was one of three Navy cruisers, with *Achilles* and *Exeter*, which engaged the German ship in the South Atlantic.

Though outgunned in the shooting by the *Graf Spee's* 11-inch armament, the Navy ships forced *Graf Spee* to seek shelter in the port of Montevideo, in neutral Uruguay, for repairs to its battle damage. But when the warship came out again she was scuttled by her captain rather than face the waiting Royal Navy.

In Britain, newspaper headlines cheered the first notable victory of the war. *Ajax* suffered damage and some loss of life in the battle but Lieutenant Deverill's recall from retirement had contributed to the war effort.

A NEW FAMILY

New year 1940 brought a big emotional commitment for Ernest Deverill. He was engaged to be married. His fiancée was Joyce Burgis, the daughter of a well-to-do farming family in Docking. For the Deverills it was a double celebration: Derek had just become engaged to Portsmouth girl, Olive Passmore-Thomas. The two announcements appeared together in the *Portsmouth Evening News*.

Joyce Burgis was 23, tall with auburn hair. She and her sister Rita, two years younger, were the daughters of Richard and Blanche Burgis of North Farm. Their older brother, John, married his fiancée, Vivienne, that January and lived some distance away. John was a master butcher but, with the coming of war, had enlisted in the Army Tank Corps. Ernest was a regular visitor to the Burgis family, who called him "Dev".

The Burgises were "a good churchgoing family" who held a prominent position in the community with a long record of public service. "Dick" Burgis, in his late fifties, served on the parish council, and on the rural district council whose offices were in Docking. He was now a wartime Special Constable; and wore the badge of an ARP warden[54] whose duties included checking that homes in the village were fully blacked out at night.

Blanche was secretary of the local branch of the District Nursing Association, which offered home visits to provide essential healthcare for low-income families. Doing their rounds by bicycle or pony and trap, these specially trained nurses acted as general nurse, midwife and health visitor for a subscription "of a few coppers a week".

Mr and Mrs Burgis had married in 1912. Blanche grew up in a large farmhouse in the nearby village of Sedgeford. Many years later she recalled that beside her home ran a wide chalk stream. In its clear waters "trout were swimming idly to and fro, or just lying in the sunshine flicking their tails".

On Sundays the couple went to church at St Mary's, the parish church where Dick Burgis was churchwarden. A fair amount of the produce displayed at Harvest Festival – sheaves of corn and vegetables – came from the farm. A big bakery in the village provided the plaited loaves.

Like their mother, the children were schooled at home by a governess. Then they were sent away to boarding school, as were children of similar background locally. In a field near the church the family kept a horse for riding. They were "a cut above us", as a villager put it.

The two sisters had very different temperaments. Joyce possessed an easy charm and was "a bit classy, a little bit reserved", one villager recalled. She worked as one of the clerks at Docking Food Office as rationing was brought in by the government on January 8 1940, starting with bacon, butter and sugar.

Church was well attended for the two Sunday services and Joyce sang in the 20-strong choir. She was captain of the 1st Docking Girl Guides, also a keen tennis player with friends on the tennis court in the garden. Rita, 21, was "confident and competent" and "bossy"; the milder Joyce was often her target, according to the family. Rita's plans did not include a quiet, comfortable marriage in Norfolk. She wanted a more exciting future elsewhere and may already have left home for London.

It is not known where Joyce and Ernest first met but "Rita may have had something to do with it", a friend recalled. The couple probably met in Docking or in Hunstanton (spoken as "Hunston" locally) the seaside town eight miles away.

Dev and Joyce were a sociable couple at the Le Strange Arms in Old Hunstanton, where the bar manager welcomed Bircham's young airmen as if they were her sons and baked cakes for them. Many were just 18 to 20 years old. "What have you got in the kitchen tonight, Mum?" they asked. They belted out rude songs in the blackout. Evenings in the bar helped them briefly to forget the strains of war revealed in their faces.

Other haunts popular with Bircham's airmen were The Railway and King William in Docking village and The Norfolk Hero at Stanhoe – the closest to the aerodrome. The "Hero" was an old, deeply rural public house renamed in honour of Horatio Nelson and said to be haunted. The walls of its two public rooms were stained yellow-brown from generations of tobacco smoke. Drinks were served through a small hatch: the airmen clubbed together to buy beer by the bucket and dipped in to fill their glasses.

The regimented, mostly male life in the RAF had been Ernest Deverill's experience since he was 15. His welcome into the Burgis family as he and Joyce anticipated marriage was, therefore, an extraordinary change that provided the warmth of a home. And of a community entirely different to those he knew.

January 1940 brought another new experience. He learned to fly a new reconnaissance aircraft that was due to replace the squadron's Ansons. The Lockheed Hudson, an American machine ordered by the British Purchasing Commission, was being transported to the UK as deck cargo in Atlantic convoys. Three Coastal Command squadrons were already flying them on operations after completing the conversion course at RAF Silloth, in the north of England. The pilots of 206 squadron were due to be sent on the course shortly.

Deverill first flew in a Hudson at Bircham in mid-December. This, with a second familiarisation flight three days later, was his introduction to this intriguing machine. On January 6 he went up as second pilot at Silloth with the unit's commander and chief flying instructor, Squadron Leader Rankin, "an Australian of exceptional keenness".

At Silloth he put in many practice landings with an instructor. He also made one-hour cross-countries from Silloth to RAF Ringway, close to Manchester, where a second Hudson conversion base was being set up.

On January 30 he made his first solo flight in the American aircraft. It was a world away from Bircham and his fiancée in Norfolk.

PAST AND FUTURE

At 240 feet above sea level Docking was (and is) one of the highest villages in Norfolk, as was demonstrated by an incident at the railway station in January 1923. A goods train of 16 trucks – three full of cattle – was being shunted out of the siding when, "with a strong wind behind them", the trucks began to roll on the gradient.

They rattled eastwards downhill out of sight and through two stations at up to 50mph before drawing to a stop more than seven miles away, newspapers reported. The cattle were unharmed, it was said.

With its mix of cottages, houses, shops and two Nonconformist chapels Docking was neither picturesque nor plain. Village school and parish church stood at the junction of the two principal streets. Scattered along them was a variety of businesses that served both the village and surrounding area: grocers, bakers, ironmonger, blacksmiths and wheelwrights, harness and saddle maker, post office, garage, watchmaker, and four public houses. A department store sold everything from groceries to linoleum and drapery, and mixed its own tea.

North Farm was one of the half dozen large farms in the district, its fields extending northwards towards the sea. The farmhouse, of weathered red brick and flint, was one of several within the village and more than 300 years old. It had been occupied by the Burgis family for at least 200 years; Burgises had worked in the area through Queen Victoria's reign as millers and butchers as well as farmers. "Dick" Burgis grew up in this house in the 1890s, with five brothers and three sisters, before taking over the farm tenancy early in the new century.

The house frontage was cloaked with ivy that strayed on to the windows, while ragged green-black holly trees flanked the path from the road to a modest porch. According to ancient lore, holly planted near a home gives protection against lightning strikes and evil influences through the cycle of the year.

In a book about the traditions of farming, published in 1934, the artist and writer Thomas Hennell painted a word picture of "a farmhouse of the old sort". He could have been describing this place when he wrote: "The whole house-front has a somewhat conventional and forlorn air, as if it exists for the sake of respectability rather than for use and pleasure. Indeed this entrance is not the one that is generally used; so we had perhaps better go round to the back."[55]

North Farmhouse was indeed "of the old sort", and the back door, sheltered by an ironwork porch, its most regular entrance. Visitors stepped first into the scullery, whose floor of rose-pink brick was sunken with age. A well in this room supplied the house with water, hand-pumped daily to the upstairs bathroom. A door led into the large kitchen with its big wooden table. Adjacent to the kitchen was the dining room and a comfortable sitting room.

Two flights of stairs showed the way up to half a dozen bedrooms, since the original building had been added to more than once in the forgotten past. Yet the past stayed mysteriously alive in this home, its rooms breathed a timeless atmosphere of calm and stillness. To sit quietly in the kitchen or sitting room was to sense the voices of past generations whispering from the walls.

Beyond the garden stood the yards and rambling cart

sheds where the farm wagons, tumbrils, ploughs and harrows were stored. A row of stables housed eight or nine broad-backed Shire horses – "gentle giants" – since little of the heavy work on the farm was mechanised.

Before the war the village was a community barely disturbed by the talk of people in the street, church clock tolling the hours and the drone of passing aircraft from Bircham Newton. The means of transport for most was the railway, pony and trap, or by bicycle – the Burgises were one of the few families in the district who owned a car. As a villager joked: "In them days, if you saw one car then that wuz busy, if you saw two you thought you wuz in London."

Work in the fields of North Farm, typical of farm work across the country, had changed little over many generations. Twenty farmworkers – men and sometimes boys not long out of school – wore old jackets, caps and trousers. In all weathers, they ploughed the fields with horse teams, cut winter cabbages for market, sowed and brought in the summer harvest, cut back hedges with billhooks, all work according to the season.

Daily orders for the men were given by the foreman, who paid out their wages on Friday evenings at his cottage. One of these men, Arthur Harrison, who started in 1940 as a 14-year-old, recalled that Dick Burgis was regarded as a decent boss. "On hot days, he would bring water from the yard for the horses in the fields if they were there all day."

A steam traction engine arrived each year on contract for the corn harvest, gently chuff-chuffing to power the big wooden threshing machine. Women and children from the village helped in the fields to bring the corn in and build the hay ricks. Tractors, although noisy, had been the coming thing for 20 years, but many farmers believed horses were more useful and less trouble. But, in a sign of the times, across Norfolk many fine traction engines already lay abandoned and rusting "in the bramble hedge".

At Docking Hall lived another significant figure in the village. By her position, Mrs Margery Hare, principal landowner in the district, also oiled the wheels in the community. A widow of four years, she was adapting to the upheavals of war – not least that a number of WAAFs (Women's Auxiliary Air Force) were billeted upstairs in her home. Her willingness to fix things where she could earned respect among villagers.

A third key figure was the Reverend Frederick Ward, vicar of St Mary's, who occupied the brooding Victorian Gothic rectory, hidden from the road by trees. He lived there with his wife and their two children and live-in cook/maid. The window of his study by the front door looked on to the drive, giving a timely view of approaching visitors.

From this room the vicar managed the enduring business of the parish: births, marriages and deaths and much more. When the time came, he would conduct Joyce and Ernest's marriage service. After four years at St Mary's he was well-liked by his parishioners, and appreciated even more by those sitting near the lectern at his services. His predecessor was remembered for showering spittle over those in the nearest pews while giving his sermons.

Life in Docking conformed to the social codes of the time by which the different classes co-existed – farm and granary workers, bakers, shopkeepers and publicans; professional people such as the tenant farmers; and the tier of landed families – yet all were interdependent. Mutual respect, and small kindnesses rendered from time to time, especially by the better placed, helped to maintain an orderly state of things.

This was the new community Ernest found himself in when he went into the village, a total contrast from his life at the aerodrome. Sometimes Dev appeared in church for Sunday service in his "civvies" – jacket and flannel trousers. He also was introduced to the Burgises' farming relatives and professional friends, for Richard and Blanche liked to entertain at home.

Among their close friends were Jack and Molly Marshall, with two young children, who moved into the village some years earlier. Jack Marshall was clerk to the district council and he and Ernest became good friends. Yet the roar of aircraft close by, day and night, was a reminder of Ernest's service duties.

A STRANGE MACHINE

Parked on the concrete apron at RAF Ringway in the last week of March 1940, the twin-engine Hudsons in camouflage drab had a chubby yet purposeful appearance. The Hudson appeared to be an aircraft in no particular hurry to fly, yet even a brief inspection showed it was a very modern aeroplane.

Under Squadron Leader Rankin, the Hudson "flying circus" – officially Coastal Command No.1 Operational Training Unit with 20 dual-control Hudsons – had set up A Flight at Ringway in the new year. It occupied two new hangars plus workshops, with airmen's accommodation in barracks.

On March 27, Sgt Deverill was posted to Ringway, on probably its second conversion course there. His competence in flying the Hudson was confirmed the next day, when Sqn Ldr Rankin assessed and qualified him as a "First pilot (day)". The 10-day course was "well-planned", and essential to learn the technical aspects of this new aircraft. It included 30 hours of lectures on engines and airframe, aircraft handling on the ground as well as flying exercises.

The camouflaged terminal building a short distance from the hangars was a reminder that, briefly before the war, the aerodrome was Manchester's new airport. "Between flights the place took on the air of a country club: afternoon teas were served in the restaurant, the airline staff resumed their game of cricket".[56]

In the ground lectures a strong emphasis was put on learning complete familiarity with the Hudson's electrical and hydraulic systems. This was so that crews would be capable of managing faults or battle damage in the air.

Technically, the Lockheed Hudson was "strange in many ways and took a bit of getting used to", one pilot summed up. It was an all-metal machine, adapted by the manufacturer from its 14-seat airliner the Lockheed 14. The designers in California had retained the passenger windows, upholstered seats and efficient heating system. The two 1,100hp Wright Cyclone radial engines, tapered wings for speed and gun turret near the twin tail, were distinctive features.

A maximum speed of about 250mph made the Hudson 60mph faster than the Anson. It could stay in the air for seven hours, giving a range of 1,900 miles. This was an aircraft in an entirely new class.

Entry to the cabin was through the bulbous rear door, which housed a dinghy in case of ditching. The cabin was roomy (the size of a large garden shed) and fitted with racks for bombs and other stores, also a fold-down rest bed. At the rear was an Elsan chemical lavatory, a luxury on an RAF plane in 1940.

The pilot sat in the usual position to port, facing a display of almost 100 dials, gauges and switches. At his right hand a console sprouted controls that included the throttle and flap levers. He also had a Sperry autopilot, another item of equipment not yet found on British aircraft. A powerful hydraulic system that operated the wing flaps, turret and undercarriage was a big advance.

There could be no doubt about the Hudson's complexity. To start each engine the pilot had to push the priming button, then the starter and booster buttons together. The ignition had to be switched on with the propeller turning – a task generally acknowledged to require three hands not two. In flight, tasks included managing the fuel mixture for each engine, and monitoring the amount of fuel in the four petrol tanks to maintain the aircraft's stability. Pilots also had two fixed machine guns in the nose to fire in battle, and could drop the bombs.

The second pilot/navigator's position, with a chart table, was down some steps in the nose. This had plenty of observation windows although the pilot's boots projected into the compartment. The main bomb-release switches were here since the second pilot was the main bomb aimer as well as navigator.

The wireless operator's desk was behind the pilot separated by a half-partition. Wireless operators, trained as wireless op/air gunners, could take over the guns in the turret if necessary.

The twin .303 machine guns in the Boulton Paul turret were the Hudson's main defence. Sitting atop the fuselage in his Perspex-glazed cupola, the gunner had a commanding all-round view as the eyes of the aircraft. And an impressive field of fire.

Movement of the guns was powered by a hydro-mechanical motor operated with a small joystick. It could elevate them 60 degrees, depress 45 degrees and traverse the turret a full 360 – rotating on 200 ball bearings. If the hydraulic power failed, the gunner could pull a small lever to disengage the motor, then rotate the turret with a crank handle to train his guns manually.

To reach his position from the cabin in full flying kit was not easy. He had to step on the Elsan, duck under a bulkhead, then squeeze upwards in the confined space, past the footrests and ammunition boxes. To exit, he had to "park the guns" facing astern and reverse the process.

Wright Cyclones were reliable engines that ran up with

a noisy, reassuring roar. On the take-off run, the aeroplane seemed to require "willpower from the pilot" to help it leave the ground. Once safely airborne "a short upward movement to the undercart lever was quickly followed by a satisfying *'clunk'… 'clunk'* as each main wheel in turn locked up".[57]

The Lockheed Hudson was demanding to fly because of its handling peculiarities, which were very different to the docile Anson. Throttles and rudders had to be used with care while taking off to keep the aircraft straight on the runway. Failing to do this might start a serious swing which, if not corrected, could result in a ground loop that wrecked the undercarriage, or worse.

Landings equally required care and practice. To compensate for its modest wing area the Hudson had impressively large "barn door" flaps, which ran out behind the wings on tracks. These increased the effective wing area, slowing the landing speed to a manageable 70mph, about that of the Spitfire fighter. There were some stark warnings in the Pilot's Notes:

Flaps to be lowered with caution, not more than 70 per cent when landing, to avoid excessive drag. Too much flap can result in dangerously low airspeed, making a go-around – if it's necessary – impossible.

At the stall with undercarriage and flaps up the aeroplane drops a wing sharply. Recovery is easy provided the control column is put forward at once; otherwise a spin will develop.

Silloth's coastal position on the Solway Firth provided wide spaces to practice circuits with an instructor before going solo. A tall brick flour mill by the seafront made a useful landmark. Increasingly advanced exercises included low flying, night flying and cross-countries to build confidence in the aircraft.

The Hudson flew well, was surprisingly manoeuvrable and quite capable on one engine, students found. One pilot declared: "They're comfortable to fly in, with plenty of space to move about, and there are practically no draughts."

As chief instructor, Rankin flew a number of times with each pilot to assess their progress. As one who trained on a previous course put it: "We all had great respect for the Hudson with its power, quick stall, powerful flaps, etc. Everything about it was bigger and faster and more powerful than anything we were used to and it took time to come to terms with it."

The course ended on April 8. Sgt Deverill's rating on Hudsons as a day captain was "Average". He would gain his full rating for night flying after building experience in the aircraft as a second pilot on squadron service.

It must have been with some satisfaction that he reported back at Bircham Newton in his best blue. His training showed that the Hudson was "not a machine for the careless or the ham-fisted", a reputation it was gaining already. But there was no doubt that, with its advanced features, good performance – plus the Elsan – it was an aeroplane of the future.

Over the next few weeks Sgt Deverill was building hours in the role of second pilot as new Hudsons arrived and were put into service. During April, the aircraft were equipped with ASV, an early air to sea-surface radar, to aid the detection of ships and submarines.

First and second pilots in the Hudsons would swap positions during sorties to give the second pilot experience of being in command. To reach the Fresians from Bircham was now only about an hour's flying, allowing a longer patrol there of perhaps four hours.

These extended periods near the enemy coast increased the risk from flak and German aircraft. Even so, there were reasons for confidence on the squadron. Then came an incident that brought home just what the crews were up against.

LUCKY TO GET BACK

The early hours of May 3 1940 started like so many others. Two crews were woken for "another damn recco", this time off the Elbe estuary. Pilot Officer Raymond Kean, Deverill, Sgt Dennis Mannion as wireless operator, and LAC Ernest Townend, gunner, were rostered for N7319.

In near darkness they were taken to their aircraft weighed down as usual with flying kit and carrying the pigeon basket, to send a message back if they ditched.

Take-off was at 3.45am. They set course eastward across the North Sea to meet the dawn. Kean was at the controls, at 5.45am, near the island of Borkum when they spotted an enemy merchant vessel and headed towards it to investigate. Then three Me109s coming out of the low sun pounced on the Hudson, firing their cannon and machine guns.

Townend's .303s stuttered back as he opened fire from his turret straight away. Two or three bursts sent the leading Messerschmitt into a steep dive out of sight, smoke pouring from its engine. But as the two remaining fighters continued their attack his guns fell silent – Ernest Townend was mortally hit.

Kean dived the Hudson to sea level to prevent attacks from beneath and raced the aircraft away from the coast on emergency boost. Heaving at the controls he swung the aircraft into violent manoeuvres, skimming the waves to throw off the enemy's aim.

Using their speed advantage, the German pilots were firing from astern and the beam so Kean had no chance to bring his front guns to bear. With no defending fire from the turret either, the Hudson crew were in dire peril.

Deverill and Mannion sped to the back of the cabin and attempted to bring Townend's body down from the turret, so the guns could be fired in his place. But hampered by the aircraft's manoeuvres they could not reach up far enough to pull the hydraulics release lever. Unable to get the gunner out they had to leave him.

Kean, bleeding from a wound to his wrist, was flying for all he was worth, jinking and out-turning the attackers. But the Hudson was holed again and again, the sea below splashing with near misses. The critical burst that would send them all into the water could not be long coming. Then the firing stopped – the German pilots were out of ammunition. They closed with the Hudson and flew alongside, rocking their wings in salute before turning for home.

The aircraft was still flying, slipstream whistling through the holes, but Kean was losing blood and near collapse. Deverill was wounded in the leg although not seriously. Mannion had escaped without a scratch. Deverill took over in the pilot's seat and continued the course for home while Kean rested. Badly damaged though the Hudson was, it responded to the controls and the engines continued to run. However, Mannion could not radio for a home bearing as his set was u/s.

With the autopilot switched "on" to fly the aircraft, the second pilot and wireless operator returned to the turret. This time they succeeded in bringing Townend's body down to the cabin, where they laid the gunner on the floor wrapped in a couple of blankets.[58]

Presently, the familiar low curve of the Norfolk coastline

came into view and they reached Bircham around 8am to make an emergency landing. With the hydraulics shot up, the flaps would not lower so the aircraft had to be brought in well above normal speed. Would they make the runway without mishap? Once across the boundary hedge Deverill put the Hudson on to the grass in a good landing – then the undercarriage collapsed.

The aircraft slid to a halt on its belly and was sharply evacuated. On the ground N7319 was a shocking sight. Fuselage, both wings and engine nacelles were heavily damaged, much of the aircraft skin tattered. At the tail, the elevator, starboard fin and rudder were badly holed, as was the turret. Engines and flying surfaces had continued to function, yet it was all but impossible to comprehend how this machine stayed in the air.

By one description it "was little more than a skeleton which, by all the rules, should have crashed into the sea". Ground crew counted a total of 242 bullet holes plus 12 from cannon-shell hits. Group Captain Grey, the commanding officer at Bircham, made an inspection and declared he had "never seen anything like it".[59]

The wounds to the two pilots were treated at Station Sick Quarters but were minor, logged as "slightly injured". Administrative procedures had to be followed. Reports of the incident were given and typed up; next of kin notified; typed copy "flimsies" forwarded to RAF departments as far up as the Air Ministry itself.

During the day, meanwhile, Ernest Deverill took time to write home. His letter was direct and reassuring:

Dear Mum, just a very few lines to forestall a possible mention of name in a casualty list. Just wounded in action, only a few slight flesh wounds in the leg – although definitely in action.

I can't tell you too much in a letter, but briefly, this is what happened:

I was navigating a plane early this morning somewhere near Germany when three Me109 fighters dropped on us. We got one of them, then the gunner was killed, the pilot was wounded, I was scratched, the other two Huns ran out of ammo, and I flew the kite back.

It was shot to hell and when I 'landed' at the 'drome, it just collapsed. No more damage done. Still, we were bloody lucky to have got back. Two MEs and us with no rear gunner left and then they still didn't get us. Anyway, I'll let you know or maybe you'll hear it over the radio...

The funeral for LAC Townend, whose response in the first moments had saved his comrades' lives, was held four days later. For reasons not explained, his body was not sent home to Middlesbrough, in north-east England, for burial. He was laid to rest in a new war cemetery in Great Bircham churchyard two miles from the aerodrome.

A week later, BBC radio reported that German forces had invaded Holland, Belgium and Luxembourg. And, with the resignation of Neville Chamberlain, Winston Churchill took over as Britain's Prime Minister, as German forces continued to advance across Europe.

Using Coastal Command aircrew as maids of all work continued to exact its price. In the space of five days that month, four Hudsons took off on sorties and did not come back. Two had been sent as part of a force to bomb installations at Hamburg.

In the final week of May a desperate rescue operation began to evacuate the thousands of troops of the British

Expeditionary Force in France who were trapped on the beaches at Dunkirk. With events unfolding rapidly, 206 Squadron rostered battle flights of three aircraft, to patrol the French and Belgian coasts. Deverill, as second pilot, flew a dawn patrol there on June 29.

The rescue effort by Royal Navy vessels and "little ships", small boats, ferries and paddle steamers, was well under way against a backdrop of thick black smoke from burning oil installations. Despite the constant air attacks on the beaches this patrol had no contact with the enemy.

Two days later, 206's battle formation intervened spectacularly at Dunkirk in an air battle between Me109s and Skua naval fighters. One of the Hudson gunners, LAC "Spike" Caulfield, shot down two Messerschmitts and damaged a third, earning the DFM. On the morning of June 2, Deverill flew in the battle formation for a second time. The six machines encountered heavy anti-aircraft fire from German guns as they patrolled off the Belgian coast.

The tempo at Bircham Newton did not let up. During June, 235 Squadron flying bombers, lost four aircraft in one afternoon when a patrol over Holland was set on by Me109s. In the first week of July, two Hudsons failed to return after being despatched on a Thursday morning to carry out a rescue search. One search pilot had married a young woman from Hunstanton just a few months earlier.

In Docking village, discreet installations revealed preparations the Army made for an invasion. Concrete mortar-firing positions, a moveable road block, tank traps and small pill boxes appeared. The beach at Brancaster was just five miles away.

At North Farm, part of the garden wall was reinforced with concrete to make a defensive position. The view through its rifle loopholes was across fields through which the enemy might advance after parachuting down or landing on the beach. In the public houses local people mingled in the evenings with off-duty airmen, and soldiers from the searchlight and gun batteries defending Bircham aerodrome. The base was subject to nuisance raids by intruder aircraft.

The formal announcement that Sgt E Deverill was awarded the Distinguished Flying Medal (and Kean the Distinguished Flying Cross) appeared in newspapers in the second week of July. In the *Western Morning News* Ernest's award, "for gallantry and devotion to duty in the execution of air operations", the citation stated, was reported on the same page as a letter to the editor from a worried reader.

It said: "At a time like the present, when we are being reminded that invasion by the enemy is not only likely but imminent, is it not a matter for concern that travelling circuses continue to be allowed to encumber our West Country roads?

"Even in peacetime the traffic delay caused by these strings of enormous slow-moving vehicles is considerable, and in the event of sudden invasion might well cause indescribable confusion."[60]

Confusion on the roads was the least of their concerns for the men of 206 Squadron. The loss of LAC Townend and damage to N7319 in May was evidence of the fate likely to befall crews who did not return. And a reminder that nobody flying from Bircham Newton could expect to survive the summer.

A QUICK DECISION

By mid-July Ernest and Joyce were making urgent preparations for their wedding. Derek and Olive had married in Portsmouth six weeks earlier. And, with Joyce's brother John already married, the expected event must have been greatly anticipated by the two families. But for Dev and Joyce the increasing tempo of the war had brought the question of a marriage date to a head. The pleasures of married life might be snatched away before they could exchange wedding rings.

Church of England formalities required that the banns announcing their intention to marry had to be read in church for three weeks before the wedding could take place. However, there was another option: the couple could apply for a special licence that permitted a marriage much sooner.

So in mid-July, on the 17th, Ernest Deverill called at Docking vicarage to see the Reverend Ward. Inside the lofty hallway the airman was shown into the study. The licence application had to be made through the vicar, acting for the church Consistory Court in Norwich, an ancient jurisdiction dating from the Middle Ages.

The application form comprised a single sheet of paper. On it was typed information that "a sergeant of the Royal Air Force" and "a spinster" with her "usual place of abode in the parish of Docking" wished to marry. Ernest signed it. The licence, once granted, would enable the marriage to take place in a matter of days. By evening he was back at the aerodrome and flew the late patrol.

For best man he picked his friend Jack Marshall. This was perhaps not only for reasons of friendship. Many of the airmen Ernest knew on the squadron had been lost, so the tasks falling to his best man were probably better put in the hands of somebody with a safe job on the ground.

The two families went ahead with the wedding preparations as the reconnaissance sorties continued, the soon-to-be bridegroom flying a patrol every couple of days as usual. At the same time, 206 squadron had begun using a new satellite aerodrome at Docking for operations since it was more suitable for night take-offs and landings.

Deverill's first flight into RAF Docking was on July 11. Short transfer flights had to be made between the two aerodromes – six to ten minutes each time – as the new one had few permanent facilities. Even the officers mess was in effect a large tent. The airfield did have electricity, running water and its own sewerage system. By contrast Docking village, like many rural communities, had a few wells and standpipes in the street for water, and mostly paraffin lamps at home for lighting. The sewerage system was weekly visits by the "night cart".

In the late evening of the 23rd Sgt Deverill was rostered as second pilot to carry out a bombing raid on the Dutch/German coast. They failed to find the target in poor conditions so bombed Texel aerodrome instead, eluding the searchlights that pursued them and returning in the early hours.

That day, he called again at the vicarage. The licence application had to be re-sworn and signed a second time to take account of various hand-written corrections, which now contributed a couple of ink blots to the page. A striking feature was the pilot's distinctive signatures. His initials, EA, and D of his surname, were formed with a conventional rounded flourish, the rest a quick, barely decipherable line sweeping urgently upwards. It was the mark of somebody not given to wasting his time, or missing his sleep from the night's flying.

The wedding took place at St Mary's two days later, on Friday 26th. It was a day of unsettled weather, cloudy and thundery. A whirlwind was reported in neighbouring Lincolnshire. The marriage was a significant event for the village "attended by a large number of local residents and of the neighbouring districts", a local newspaper recorded.

One family member who could not be there was Ernest's brother, Dimps. He was at sea in the Mediterranean, serving in the Royal Navy as a chief electrical artificer.

Ernest in uniform – DFM ribbon newly sewn on his tunic – took his place at the chancel step. Joyce walked up the aisle wearing "a dress of clover bouclette smocked in lido-blue, with hat and accessories to match. Her flowers were shaded clover carnations".

Unusually for a wedding at St Mary's the choir sang at the service – women and girls on one side of the chancel, men and boys on the other. There were two hymns. One, the popular Victorian wedding hymn *O perfect Love*, was a poignant choice. Choir and congregation picked up the first verse: "*O perfect love, all human thought transcending…*" Then, as voices and organ swelled into the second verse, the words gave full expression to the occasion:

O perfect Life, be thou their full assurance
Of tender charity and steadfast faith,
Of patient hope and quiet, brave endurance,
With childlike trust that fears no pain or death.

With the marriage register signed and witnessed, the new husband and wife walked to the porch. Outside,

Docking Guides were lined up in a guard of honour, the couple being presented with lucky horseshoes. The wedding party made their way to North Farm for the reception where, in the garden, relatives clicked their cameras for the family album. "Sgt and Mrs Deverill were the recipients of many congratulatory telegrams and presents," the newspaper said.[61]

Each marriage is different, with its own possibilities in time and place. This was a love match, brought about by the war. But it was love under difficult stars.

MORE CLASHES

The satellite aerodrome at Docking was intended to deflect the Luftwaffe's attention from Bircham Newton's vital maintenance facilities. It began to be used for operations since it was both a lesser target and safer for take-offs at night.

The satellite's grass runways could cope better with the landing *thump* when loaded Hudsons touched down. At Bircham, their main wheels punched through the surface because of faults in the subsoil. This could break the undercarriage, even wreck the aircraft.

Damaged and dismantled aeroplanes that had crashed on the aerodrome or in fields were hauled through Docking to the workshops at Bircham on the RAF's 60-foot articulated trailers. These loads, with wings detached, were wide as well as long, fouling hedges along the roadside until farm workers were bought in to slash the hedges to waist height. To negotiate the village streets an airman perched on top of the fuselage wielding a pole to lift telephone wires clear.

In the south of England, Spitfire, Hurricane and Defiant squadrons continued their costly struggle against the large German bomber formations. For 206 Squadron the patrols continued as usual. With effect from August 1 Sgt Deverill was certified as First Pilot (night), making him fully qualified as a Hudson captain.

On August 5 occurred one of the needless accidents of wartime flying. A Hudson was returning at 6pm after a sea search for a crew in a dinghy when something went wrong.

Approaching Bircham to land, the aircraft stalled making a vertical turn, crashed on farmland and exploded. The four crew all perished. The pilot was Raymond Kean, the New Zealander whose skills had shaken off the deadly attack by Messerschmitts three months earlier. He was 22.

Also lost in the crash was Dennis Mannion, the wireless operator who, in May, had got away without a scratch. Next day, August 6, a Hudson crashed on landing at Docking and again the bombs blew up, but the crew got out in time.

On August 27 Ernest Deverill had another clash with the enemy. He flew an early patrol that morning and was rostered to fly again that evening at 19.45, as second pilot. At 20.30, flying at 600 feet as the light faded, they encountered a Heinkel 115 floatplane. The Heinkel made a tight climbing turn, dived on the Hudson's tail and opened fire from 400 yards.

The shooting was accurate, putting holes in the fuselage, main wing and turret, and wounding Deverill in one hand. As he reported later: "Our gunner held fire until sure of his aim and then got in two good bursts. E/A was seen diving from 250ft to approximately 20ft and although it was not seen to strike the water, owing to failing light, it is considered that it was destroyed."

They got back safely, landing at RAF West Raynham in Norfolk with a burst tyre. Deverill's injury was minor; he flew on convoy duty two days later. Yet this was a narrow escape as some of the aircraft's control cables were partly severed.

On another patrol they machine-gunned an E-boat. This must have been a calculated risk since the German torpedo boats were powerfully armed with Oerlikon anti-aircraft guns or 20mm cannon. Their lethal range extended well beyond the 400 yards at which the Hudson's machine guns were effective.

Villagers in Docking were getting used to Hudsons crash landing and exploding. Design of the Hudson's wing was a factor. The aircraft, originally intended for take-offs and landings on a concrete runway at airports, carried its fuel not in separate fuel tanks but in wing compartments – a "wet wing". A hard landing risked damage that could cause a petrol leak and fire.

One villager recalled: "At night the sky would go red, just red, where aircraft were landing and blowing up. You didn't hear anything, just saw the flash. Then, because of the time delay, you'd hear a terrific explosion."[62]

The patrols continued normally that autumn as the threat of invasion receded, the squadron's losses easing. Often there was nothing to report from the patrols. Deverill's growing experience as a full captain raised the chances that he could survive his full tour with 206. Then at the beginning of October he was promoted, from Sergeant to Flight Sergeant (temporary).

On November 7, the squadron flew 300 miles south-west to Cornwall on detachment to the Coastal Command station at St Eval. Coastal Command was overstretched, so Hudson squadrons were sent there in turn to keep up reconnaissance patrols off the coast of western France.

St Eval was in a wrecked state when 206 arrived, with damaged buildings and many broken windows. The station had been attacked frequently since the summer by bombers and fighters attempting to stop its activities. Living conditions therefore were poor, with the airmen having to sleep on straw palliasses.

Next day, Flt Sgt Deverill was sent across the English Channel to carry out a "photo recco" of Lorient, in

Brittany, where the U-boat base at the port was being expanded. But freezing winter air temperatures forced him to return because the aircraft was icing up. He returned to Bircham after ten days.

On November 19, he flew as first pilot on a recco off the Dutch coast, between the ports of Emden and Rotterdam. The crew went into action, encountering flak, when they "shot up a Jerry convoy".

This was Ernest's final sortie in a momentous tour. A note in the logbook written by his C.O., Wing Commander John Constable-Roberts, summarised: "109 operational trips of a total time of approx 360 hours. About 45,000 miles!!" The final flying assessment reads: "As a General Reconnaissance pilot: Above Average." It would be hard to argue with that.

SENT TO INSTRUCT

Ernest Deverill's new posting, after some leave, was another step forward. He arrived at No.2 Central Flying School at RAF Cranwell on December 9 or 10 to train as a flying instructor. Before the war, instructors were sent there on a nine-week course. It had since been squeezed into four weeks because the RAF needed many more instructors.

He was taught the art of instructing in two different aircraft: the Avro Tutor and Airspeed Oxford. The Tutor, a two-seat biplane, was a standard RAF initial trainer during the mid-1930s, so this was a return to old-fashioned open-cockpit flying, in order to teach on Tiger Moths.

Oxfords were now the standard advanced trainer. The "Ox-box", as widely known, was well fitted out with controls and instruments so that pilots, navigators, bomb aimers and wireless operators could practice their roles together.

Taking to the skies in an open-cockpit aeroplane that winter was not ideal. Over the four weeks conditions varied from fair to rain and fog, with snow in early January.

A key skill Ernest had to learn was the instructing patter. This had to be synchronised with each manoeuvre of the aircraft. "You have to describe what's happening exactly as it happens, not a second sooner or later." Coached by his instructor, patter had to be practised while taxying and in the air until totally fluent, including during aerobatics.

He was signed off the course on January 10 "qualified to instruct on multi-engine types". His rating: "Average".

What befell Portsmouth on the night of January 10/11 1941 was grim. The dockyard and town had been bombed frequently since August 1940 but this was a devastating raid: German bombing changed the city landscape. Many people were killed and thousands made homeless; though as before, the northern suburbs were mostly spared.

Two waves of aircraft carried out the attack, starting major fires with bombs and incendiaries. Water to fight the fires ran desperately short because water mains had fractured. Power was cut across the city when the generating station was hit.

The three principal shopping streets were destroyed, as was a hospital, cinemas and a theatre. Among the landmarks lost was The George Hotel and with it Nelson's bedroom which the hotel had preserved for more than 130 years.

The Guildhall stood a blackened shell. Despite the efforts of the fire watch, an incendiary had set the building alight. It burned through the night and the next day, "ribbons of green fire" dropping from the clock tower as its copper roof tiles melted.

In Southsea, many homes and shops were burned out. And Chivers school, where Ernest and Derek laboured to pass their exams, was gone. The former pupil F E Wooden recalled "in the early smoke-filled daylight walking down to Cottage Grove on my way to work… and seeing the smoke still rising from the ruins of our old school. Only the lower parts of the walls were standing". Further on, Kings Road "was impassable with flames roaring across the road from one side to the other".

However, the school was still functioning. Within days, masters moved the pupils to the church halls at St Bartholomew's a few streets away and restarted classes. Meanwhile, many people in Portsmouth had had enough. They were sleeping outside the city and travelling in to work each day.

TRICKY TO TEACH

On January 13 1941, Flt Sgt Deverill was posted as an instructor to the Polish Flight Training School (PFTS) at RAF Hucknall, near Nottingham. Many Polish pilots and ground crew had escaped to England, through France and by various other routes, when the war began.

Polish pilots fought with great distinction in the Battle of Britain, with 303 Polish Squadron in particular achieving high scores against the German formations, with some winning the DFC.

They also had to adapt to the British way of life: to milky tea, warm beer, fish-paste sandwiches and poorly heated homes. Now, the RAF was training the pilots formally in its methods and disciplines before posting them to new squadrons.

As a "rest" from operations Deverill's new posting brought extra demands. In particular, it was necessary to ensure that these men, whose command of English varied, learned the standard procedures, in English, that were essential for communicating in the air. After some initial dual flights instructing on the Tiger Moths, Ernest was switched to the unit's Airspeed Oxfords, to provide multi-engine training.

Instructing always had its risks, as an incident in March showed. During a dual exercise, for a reason unknown, Ernest's pupil put the Oxford down in a field. This could have been over-enthusiasm while carrying out a practice forced landing, which required picking a field, making an approach and climbing away again.

Finding that they were in a muddy field, Deverill as instructor had two options. He could ask for a recovery team to come and transport the machine back to Hucknall (with some explaining to do), or fly the Oxford out himself. He opted to fly it out.

This required a careful assessment. Clinging mud could make it impossible to reach flying speed or clear any obstacles, as the aircraft had to accelerate to 65mph IAS (indicated air speed) to leave the ground. Nevertheless the take-off was successful. "I frightened myself", he noted in his logbook.

At the end of the month he was posted from general instructing to the unit's testing and grading flight. His judgments therefore helped to decide the trainees' suitability to be bomber or fighter pilots.

On April 1 1941, Ernest Deverill was promoted to temporary Warrant Officer. This was a marked step up in his career as it was the highest non-commissioned rank. It also gives an insight into the RAF's view of his capabilities at that time. As King's Regulations stated:

The qualities required of warrant officers are self-reliance, initiative and resource, together with tact, firmness and judgment in dealing with men. Technical warrant officers must have wide technical knowledge and experience.

On May 7 came a major turning point in his RAF career. He was granted a commission, "For the duration of hostilities" as the official wording put it. The promotion gave Ernest a new identity in the service, one that crossed the social divide. And it answered the unspoken question at interview: "Will he be one of us?"

This change of status followed standard procedure:

Warrant Officer Deverill was discharged from the RAF on May 6 and re-appointed next day as Pilot Officer Deverill. And given a new service number.

His basic pay rose to just over £25 a month. When the commission came through he had to buy a new uniform and kit, purchasing these with an RAF allowance during a short leave. Commonly this involved a visit to London, where officers' clothing was available in outlets ranging from gentlemen's tailors in the West End, such as Gieves of Old Bond Street ("Outfitter to the Royal Air Force"), to high-street clothing firms that included Burtons and Horne Brothers.

The allowance had to pay for a new tunic and peaked service cap, shirts, collars and tie, a greatcoat, shoes, socks and other items The new clothes brought a welcome end to 10 years of wearing scratchy serge – an officer's tunic was made of soft barathea cloth.

With its new officers in wartime coming from unusually varied backgrounds, many men had to spend carefully to obtain their new uniform. As Kay Carroll, the wing commander's wife, had observed: "Wealthy people are rare birds in the Air Force."

A bomber pilot recalled how he went about buying his new kit: "I opened an overdraft with the Westminster Bank and travelled by the crowded train to London... I bought the cap, tunic, trousers and greatcoat from Burtons for £25; the raincoat cost £3 at Burberrys; and Horne's provided the shirts and socks, with some bits and pieces, for £12 7s 1d [£12.35]. The pilot's wings I drew from stores for nothing."[63]

As a pilot officer Ernest Deverill was earning more, but instead of free meals he now had monthly mess bills to pay for his food and drink. It was a strict rule that failure to settle the bill promptly each month would result in an inquiry. However, the privileges he gained were the facilities of the officers mess and the services of a batman (shared with several other officers) to tidy his room, organise laundry and bring an early morning cup of tea.

There also were rules on officers' general behaviour that could be enforced by their commander. As King's Regulations stated: "A C.O. will, by advice and timely intervention, endeavour to prevent disputes. He will discountenance any disposition in his officers to gamble or to indulge in extravagant expenditure. He will check any tendency among his officers to practical jokes."

Not that this prevented a good commander from turning a blind eye to noisy larks and games in the mess – even joining in – as his fit young men let off steam.

Deverill continued at Hucknall through May and June. In July, he was instructing in the single-engine Fairey Battle, a retired warhorse from 1940. But then his rest period ended and the next phase of his career beckoned. He would be flying bombers.

GOOD LUCK AND BAD

On August 5 1941 Pilot Officer Deverill was posted to No.25 Operational Training Unit at RAF Finningley, in Yorkshire, to crew up for operations in Bomber Command. Typically, this was a casual business in which the airmen assembled in a hangar and mingled until, by a mix of chance, hunch and good judgment, they chose each other. The aircraft at 25 OTU were Vickers Wellingtons, the reliable twin-engine aircraft Bomber Command was depending on until four-engine bombers reached the squadrons in greater numbers.

In the last week of September Ernest Deverill and his new crew were posted from the OTU to 97 Squadron at RAF Coningsby in Lincolnshire. The squadron, under Wing Commander Denys Balsdon, was flying the new Avro Manchester, the RAF's latest bomber.

This was a large twin-engine machine with front, rear, and mid-upper gun turrets, a huge bomb bay and a large amount of room for crews by previous standards. On September 27 Ernest was signed off as a bomber pilot. His rating: "Above average".

However, it was not easy to build flying hours in the Avro Manchester. The aircraft had given trouble since entering service and efforts to put the problems right continued. The biggest issue was its Rolls-Royce Vulture engines, which were failing to give the amount of power expected. Take-offs could be an alarming experience in which a loaded aircraft barely scraped into the air.

The engines were worryingly unreliable. This complex

24-cylinder unit, comprising two 12-cylinder engines on a common crankcase, had gone into service too early. The design and lubrication of the crankshaft big-end bearings was causing engines to break up and catch fire. In some cases, pistons and connecting rods burst through the crankcase while a Manchester was revving up on the ground.

Trouble also came from its hydraulic system. The pumps, jacks and valves controlling the aircraft's flaps, bomb doors and other vital functions were connected by more than 200 feet of tubing, with numerous joints. This system of pressure and return pipes, which ran the full length of the fuselage, was prone to leaks, air locks and blockages – a plumber's nightmare.

Further, the Manchester's 90-foot wingspan gave insufficient lift for a machine with an all-up weight of 50,000lbs. As one pilot said: "The overall result was that the aircraft would not fly high enough with a full load. They could 'stagger' up to around 16,000 feet before finally running out of steam.

"As soon as the power was reduced for cruising speed, the aircraft slowly lost height to around 12,000 feet."[64] This made the Manchester a fair target for German flak, while getting back to England if an engine failed over Europe was down to luck.

Rolls-Royce were working to remedy the Manchester's engine problems, while Avros tried to resolve the issues with the hydraulic system. The aircraft also had sluggish directional stability, which made it slow in turns. The cause of this was the aeroplane's twin fins and rudders, which were too small.

Some months later at Coningsby, Wing Commander Guy Gibson, the energetic new commander of 106

Squadron, apparently was more relaxed about flying the Manchester. According to his book Enemy Coast Ahead: "The take-off seemed to take hours and the turns were so slow that it felt almost unreal. But she was smooth enough at 180 miles an hour, so long as her engines kept running."[65]

For better or worse, this was the aircraft Deverill had to fly. Meanwhile, he was experiencing life on one of the RAF's top bomber squadrons. As a civilian who visited bomber stations observed in 1941:

Air warfare entails a lot of waiting about, and figures are always to be seen loitering unoccupied around the airfield. In the [officers] mess, at almost any hour of the day, one or two men can be found lounging about, writing a letter or glancing at the paper. But soon, one looks at his watch and silently goes out.[66]

However, the RAF was radically changed from the "all-male" organisation Ernest Deverill had entered 10 years earlier. Increasing numbers of women of the WAAF, from different social backgrounds, were working at the bomber stations and elsewhere. They were to be seen in offices and workshops, in a rising number of trades, after specialist training. Women could enlist from the age of 17½ but some joined up much younger, down to girls of 14, after hiding their age.

Trades open to WAAF recruits ranged from cook, signals clerk, wireless operator, radar plotter, to aircraft fitter, parachute packer and barrage balloon crew. Also, sparking-plug tester, batwoman, intelligence officer, weather staff, cypher officer and photographer.

Out on the aerodromes, women worked as engine and

airframe mechanics, who went on flight tests with aircrew. Some were the "instrument bloke" at dispersals repairing aircraft altimeters, fuel and oil-pressure gauges. Others drove staff cars, crew coaches, trucks and the tractors hauling loaded bomb trolleys from bomb stores to the aircraft.

Airmen were forbidden to enter WAAF accommodation, at least beyond the anteroom, while the messing system ensured the social separation between officers and ranks was maintained.

Many women who went out with aircrew had to cope with the loss of someone who failed to return. A semi-official account of the time explained:

"Shattered lives there are in the WAAF but with rare exceptions, including the casualties of air attacks, eyes have become brighter and carriages more upright. Hours of exercise and country air have had their effect.

"Wrapped round by discipline and the friendship that is no small part of service life, surely all are venturing into a more spacious world than they had imagined."[67]

On November 1, Ernest Deverill was signed off by his C.O. as a qualified first pilot on Manchesters. A week later on November 8 the crew, in A Flight, were sent on their first operation to bomb the docks at Dunkirk on the French coast. The crews of three aircraft from the flight were briefed for the trip. But Deverill's tour got off to a desperate start.

They took off in Manchester K-King at 17.45 with Pilot Officer Hodge, a Rhodesian new from the training unit, flying as second pilot. Donald Hodge had already done one "second dickey" trip since arriving on the squadron.

He was flying the aircraft as they made the run-up to the target at 13,000 feet. They were met by searchlights and a fierce flak barrage when, from a close burst, shrapnel smashed into the cockpit. Hodge was hit and seriously wounded, sending the aircraft into a dive as he slumped over the controls. They lost height rapidly until Deverill was able to take over and pull out at 4,000 feet. Hodge, losing blood, was taken to the rest bed.

The aircraft also was in a poor state. The bomb doors were stuck open, the interior lights on and could not be switched off. They had to turn back. In short order Deverill dumped some of the bombs, the rest in the North Sea on the way home. Returning to Coningsby he made a successful crash-landing and the stricken second pilot was taken to the Station Sick Quarters. Donald Hodge died there at 11pm. Next morning the full extent of the damage to the aircraft was revealed, showing holes in both the fuselage and wings.

His funeral took place four days later at Coningsby Cemetery, next to the airfield boundary. It was conducted in the afternoon by the squadron chaplain. Hodge was buried with full military honours; his family in Rhodesia, who had been notified of his death, arranged a wreath.

Deverill attended the service at the graveside with several fellow officers, a detachment of WAAFs and the firing party with their rifles. All were wearing their greatcoats to keep out the cold. As King's Regulations prescribed for funerals: "The attending party will consist of as many officers and airmen of the unit as may be desirous of attending and can be spared from their duties."

The firing party loosed their volleys by the graveside and the group dismissed to return to the station. Later that month, in a letter to the Air Council in London, Donald Hodge's mother wrote: "We are very bruised but proud to know he gained a life's wish – to be a pilot in the Royal Air Force."

Pilot Officer Deverill's second trip was on the night of December 7/8, an attack on Aachen in Holland, to wreck the "Nazi party HQ", the record says. But they did not get there. The aircraft's guns failed when the gunners tested them over the North Sea, forcing a decision to turn back.

His third op came on December 18. Deverill's crew was one of 11 briefed to raid Brest in western France, to bomb the battleships *Scharnhorst*, *Gneisenau* and *Prinz Eugen* berthed in the harbour for repairs, after marauding shipping in the Atlantic. It would be an understatement to call this a dangerous mission: it was to be a daylight raid, the ships were heavily defended by flak guns and German fighters. Leading from the front, Wing Commander Balsdon decided to go on this raid, putting himself down to fly with Flt Sgt Pendrill's crew.

It was a formidable task to take on. Many earlier attacks by the RAF had limited success. Take-off was at about 9.30am, with Deverill in F-Freddie. But again a technical problem rendered his aircraft "u/s" and his was one of two that turned back. Most crews were back at Coningsby by mid-afternoon, two landing away because of the poor weather. Then events turned black. A radio message to Control from Pendrill and Balsdon informed the duty staff that they had serious damage from flak and a wounded gunner on board.

A crowd collected at the control tower to watch as the Manchester appeared and made its approach "his elevators shot off, or most of them". However, the approach was too high. As it crossed the airfield, the big aircraft pitched up, gained some height and stalled, engines roaring in a doomed attempt to go round. In full view it plunged into the middle of the aerodrome and burst into flames. Nothing could be done.

The new squadron C.O., appointed just before Christmas, was Wing Commander Jack Kynock. To him fell the headache of keeping the squadron's unreliable aircraft up to operational strength while taking on a new one that was entering squadron service. This was the Avro Lancaster, a four-engine conversion from the troublesome Manchester and replacement for it on the production line.

The first week of January 1942 landed 97 Squadron with the task of trying again to disable the German battleships berthed at Brest. The RAF had bombed these vessels in the port regularly for months, causing damage, yet the vessels were still afloat and preparing for sea.

On the night of January 9/10 it was the turn of Deverill's crew, despatched in a force of four aircraft. Thick cloud foiled the operation although one pilot, Warrant Officer Mycock, dived from 1,500 feet to 200 feet to drop his bombs.

However, Deverill did not reach Brest, nor even France. Compass trouble after take-off put his Manchester on a reciprocal course, wasting precious time flying in the opposite direction. "On discovery of error it was too late to continue to target and the aircraft returned to base," the squadron operations record noted. Mid-month, the crew were sent to Bremen as one of a force of five aircraft. But was Deverill's luck out again? There was "plenty of flak" at the target but 10/10ths cloud forced him to bring back the bombs.

On January 16 he had his first flight in the new Lancaster – 45 minutes of circuits and bumps in the four-engine aircraft that would replace the Manchester. Winter weather was now hampering operations though there was time for training on the Lancasters, which were trickling through from the factory to 44 and 97 squadrons, the first to have them.

Four Lancasters were on strength at the station by the end of the month, although by then continuous snow had stopped flying. Deverill next flew the Lancaster on February 2, his birthday, practising landings as first pilot. The need was to ensure pilots were familiar with the new bomber as quickly as possible to speed the Lancaster's entry into service.

It was two days later that Ernest Deverill was drawn by the war artist Cuthbert Orde. The War Artists Committee in London had been set up to record the war through the eyes of artists, as a separate record from photographs and film.

Exhibitions of their work in London and regional towns had put the RAF increasingly in the public eye. Now, the public relations department at the Air Ministry were keen to have portraits made of bomber pilots – by which they really meant officers.

The Ministry was seeking to raise the profile of Bomber Command to demonstrate that the RAF was important to winning the war. Some people in high places were sceptical, believing that the huge resources invested in building bombers could be better used in other ways.

Deverill's portrait will have been made in a makeshift studio, very likely at Coningsby, in the way Orde had produced his Battle of Britain pictures. Working on a short-term contract, he had drawn another 97 Squadron officer days before and had more 5 Group men to draw.

Cuthbert Orde was still doing work as a portrait painter, having produced oil paintings to commission of a number of RAF high-ups, and occasionally portraits of society people. The drawing of Ernest Deverill, however, gives an insight into the mind of a pilot in continuous service since the first day of the war. Many of his comrades were gone, two in his own crews. Another visitor to bomber stations who spent time with the pilots wrote, "... one notices that through the mask of self-control their eyes gaze out serious and preoccupied".[68]

Three days after sitting for the drawing, Deverill, with two other officers plus aircrew, flew to RAF Boscombe Down, in Wiltshire. They reported to the Intensive Flying Development Flight for a short attachment. The flight had the first two production Lancasters, L7527 and L7529, at the aerodrome for "intensive flying" by service pilots to help iron out the inevitable snags in a new aircraft. Any modifications required would be incorporated on the production line.

The Lancaster was a redesigned and strengthened version of the Manchester with four Rolls-Royce Merlin engines on a longer wing. It had taller fins and rudders, which cured the directional problem. At nearly 30 tons the Lancaster was more than two tons heavier, with a beefed-up undercarriage to cope with the extra weight.

Boscombe Down was a busy place. Other aircraft were in the queue for testing, as memos on the Lancaster from those in authority made clear. One dated February 2 said:

The object of this additional flying is to check the efficiency of the mainplane skin modification and operation of the supercharger control gear. Get this polished off as quickly as we possibly can, and release Bomber Command crews back to 5 Group.

Another memo next day urged the need to finish these tests to "clear the way for intensive flying on other types".[69]

The "mainplane skin modification" referred to a problem that had to be resolved. Extending the

Manchester wing to 102 feet to take four Merlins had worked brilliantly, allowing two further fuel tanks to be fitted, so increasing range. But in flight the top skin of the Lancaster could be seen wrinkling near the wingtips. Was the wing strong enough?

On one flight, a crew was taking off in L7527 when one of the five-foot main wheels with its telescopic leg fell away and bounced down the runway. The pilot made a neat wheels-up landing on the grass and saved the aircraft, but it was out of service until repairs and modifications could be made. Ernest Deverill's stint at Boscombe Down lasted about ten days. Meanwhile, a further memo read cautiously: "I think we are reasonably safe in allowing the Command to continue flying the Lancaster provided they maintain the daily inspection we have called for."[70]

In mid-February, a remarkable event relieved 97 Squadron from further death-defying sorties against the German battleships at Brest. *Scharnhorst*, *Gneisenau* and *Prinz Eugen* slipped out of the port at night and steamed for the North Sea hidden by mist and low cloud. British forces, in confusion, acted too late to prevent them sailing through the Dover Strait: the "Channel Dash" outwitted them.

Early in March, 97 Squadron moved from Coningsby to a satellite base at Woodhall Spa five miles away. Ground crews had to cycle between the two camps for weeks. Woodhall was a new wartime aerodrome with three long concrete runways forming a triangular pattern; the accommodation, in Nissen huts, was basic.

More new Lancasters were being delivered – "The fuselage had a smell all its own compounded of oil and dope and paint and cold metal".[71] And ground crews, backed by staff from Avros, were working to make them fit for operations. Progress was steady although the weather hampered these efforts, as the squadron record shows:

> **9.3.42 Total aircraft strength is 12 Lancasters – cross-country and local flying.**
> **15.3.42 Strength of Lancasters now 16, 9 serviceable – 6 aircraft required for ops, later cancelled and six night cross- countries detailed and carried out.**
> **17.3.42 Strength of Lancasters now 18, 9 serviceable.**
> **18.3.43 Seven aircraft for ops – cancelled due to weather.**
> **19.3.42 Five aircraft detailed and briefed for gardening ops – cancelled in the afternoon owing to weather.**

During this period Ernest Deverill was sent on 5 Group's Beam Approach Training (BAT) course at "Waddo" – RAF Waddington near Lincoln. This was to be taught the method of landing "blind" in mist and fog guided by radio signals.

There were ten pilots on the six-day course. Group was keen that all its pilots should be given this training when they could be spared from duties. Therefore, the number of Airspeed Oxfords on strength at had been raised from six to eight.

Beam Approach was a British version of the German Lorenz bad-weather landing system at European airports before the war. Waddington's BAT unit of 150 personnel included "technical bods" such as electricians and a carpenter to keep the equipment working since it could be unreliable, especially in rainy weather.

The training involved five hours of ground instruction on the Link trainer, in the Link hut, and ten flights of about an hour in the Oxfords to practice in the air. The Link trainer was an early type of flight simulator.

In the air, the pupil approached the aerodrome at 1,000 feet, under a cockpit hood, to pick up a narrow beam that indicated the runway centreline. This was heard as a radio signal in his headphones, as dots or dashes, telling him if his aircraft was right, or left, of the runway. The sounds merged to a steady tone when the pilot was flying on the centreline.

He then made turns to line up for the approach end of the runway. Two neon lights lit in turn on the instrument panel as he crossed the airfield Outer beacon, then Inner beacon, enabling him to adjust his rate of descent.

This was not exactly a blind landing. In fog conditions the method brought an aircraft down to about 300 feet, when the runway should be visible. And the manoeuvres over the airfield allowed only one aircraft at a time to use the system. Instructors could spot when a pilot was becoming fatigued from the concentration required, failing to tell dots from dashes over the runway. Deverill must have had an advantage, because of his years of radio and Morse.

Back on the squadron, on March 20 six crews were briefed again for a "gardening" sortie, to drop parachute mines in shipping lanes off the Friesian Islands. Deverill was not going but Flying Officer "Rod" Rodley was. This brought the Lancaster's wingtips problem to a head.

Rodley set off loaded with six 1,500 lb mines and full tanks: "well over maximum take-off weight", he recalled. But after leaving the runway, off track and keeping under low cloud, he found the town of Boston looming in his windscreen. He was much too low and the tower of St Botolph's church ("Boston Stump") was more than 260 feet high. He made "an atrocious turn [and] we roared across the rooftops". He and his co-pilot then were astonished to find the starboard wingtip had gone. "On the port side, a six-foot high green-and-sand tip of camouflage paint stood at right angles to the wing."[72]

Rodley steered for an emergency landing on the coast five miles away and put the aircraft wheels-up on to Freiston Sands. All got out safely, but when the tide came in the aircraft was a write-off. Avro's designers redoubled their efforts, specifying better riveting of the wing panels.

With four engines, longer wing and redesigned tail, the Avro Lancaster, as successor to the Manchester, was a transformed machine that could fly higher and further. As one pilot recalled:

Everything about it was just right. Its muscular, swept lines were beautiful to look at. It flew with effortless grace and had a precise, weighted feel. It made the pilot's job easy. You could throw it all over the skies if you had the inclination and some physical strength.[73]

Among many production changes, the hydraulic system was replaced by one less prone to leaks. According to one explanation: "The Lancaster hydraulic system is not complex but there is a lot of it."

The 12-cylinder Merlin engine has been described as "a veritable mass of gears". Its crankshaft, spinning at up to 3,000rpm, powered a maze of shafts and cogs to drive – at different speeds – the starter motor, two camshafts, two magnetos, supercharger, fuel pump, oil-pressure pump, propeller reduction gear and more. For all that it was very reliable. If an engine failed the Lancaster still flew well on three.

At the end of March 1942 a new squadron commander arrived. Wing Commander John "Boy" Collier was the same age as Deverill and, like him, had flown on operations since the first day of the war. When Collier appeared, the squadron's problems with its Manchesters, and taking on the Lancaster, were summed up by Wing Commander Kynoch, who said: "Well, I am glad you have arrived to take me out of my misery."[74]

Woodhall Spa, Collier recalled, was "a typical wartime airfield, stretching over miles of fertile Lincolnshire countryside... Living in Nissen huts in damp woods was never the happiest of environments. Even so, the good spirits of the NCOs and men was very noticeable and the complaints very few and far between".

Big bombers such as the Lancaster had a crewman working in a new RAF trade – flight engineer. His job, sitting by the pilot, was to manage the aircraft's engine, electrical and hydraulic systems, monitor fuel consumption; and assist the pilot during take-off and landings.

The teething problems plus the weather had slowed the Lancaster's readiness for operations but the situation was improving. And Deverill's crew, after one or two recent changes, had settled. By early April it was Sgt John Cooper, flight engineer; P/O Edward Butler, navigator; Sgt Ron Irons, wireless operator; Sgt Ken Mackay, mid-upper gunner; Sgt Jeffrey Devine, bomb aimer; and Flt Sgt William Keane, rear gunner.

Pilot Officer Butler's rating as a navigator was "Exceptional". Ernest was fortunate to have a "nav" he could rely on as it was vital in the air to be sure of an aircraft's position. Now the crew could only wait and see what they would be ordered to do.

ALL THERE IS TO IT

A week into April 1942 it became clear at Woodhall Spa that something was up. At Waddington the buzz was the same. Pip Beck, a WAAF radio operator in the watch office (control tower), said: "A suspicion grew in Control that something big was being laid on for sometime in the near future, and 44 would not be the only squadron involved.

"There had been frequent visits from Sqn Ldr Sherwood and Flt Lt Penman of 97 squadron, who of course reported into Control at each landing, as all visiting aircraft were required to do."[75]

Soon enough, at Woodhall Spa, Collier picked his six most experienced crews. Ernest Deverill's crew was one of them. With two further crews as reserves, all were taken off normal duties to practice formation flying.

Sherwood would lead the front section of three aircraft, and the whole formation. Deverill was put in the second section with Warrant Officer Mycock, led by Penman. Penman's Australian navigator, Pilot Officer Ifould, was possibly the best on the squadron.

On April 12 the six aircraft, plus reserves, were sent out on the first of several days of long cross-countries to practise low-level formation flying and bombing at Wainfleet range, on the Lincolnshire coast. The second section maintained position half a mile behind the leading three aircraft. Meanwhile, six crews were picked at Waddington, led by Squadron Leader Nettleton, and were carrying out the same exercises.

Sgt Churchill, a wireless operator in 44 Squadron, said: "We started with loose formation over the sea, which gradually got tighter and lower. Finally, we were flying with our wingtips overlapping just above the sea. Then we moved to flights over land, to sorties over Scotland. It was exhilarating, flying down the valleys, scattering sheep in the process.

"Now and again we flew alongside trains and, much to the amazement of the passengers, even below them where the tracks ran along an embankment."[76] These fliers from the two squadrons were at the top of their game. From 97 Squadron's log:

13.4.41 Six aircraft on formation flying with two reserves. Bomb load 4 x 1000lb dummy, 4 x11 1/2lb practice bombs. Cross-countries as detailed, bombed Wainfleet. Group Captain Rowe flew with S/L Sherwood.
14.4.41 Eight aircraft took off for formation cross-country and bombing Wainfleet with same load as yesterday.
W/C Collier flew with S/L Dugdale. Formation exercise successfully carried out – duration 5-5½ hours.
15.4.42 Bombing at Wainfleet and tests.

Mixed weather added to the hazards. Rodley, flying behind in one of the reserve aircraft, recalled that during one sortie "I saw ahead of us the [800ft] radio masts at Rugby and as far as I could tell the leading two vics hadn't seen them in the rather misty conditions." At the moment he decided to give a radio warning "the next thing I saw was six aircraft – in plan view – climbing over them!"[77]

A 5½-hour sortie routed the formation down to Selsey Bill on the South Coast, north to Scotland to make a simulated low-level attack on Inverness, then back to base. By now the crews had some idea of the task ahead, but as to the actual target, on the station there were only rumours. And despite the plan that the two squadrons would carry out the practice flights together they had not met up.

On April 17 the special crews at Woodhall were called to a briefing at 11am (and 44 Squadron at Waddington) for an operation that afternoon. When the curtain covering the wall map was pulled back, the red ribbon stretched right across France into southern Germany, ending at the city of Augsburg. There was silence, then incredulous laughter, at the very idea of attacking this distant place in enemy territory. Then Collier addressed the room: "Well, gentlemen, now you know what the target is."

The plan was to cross France in daylight at low level, to avoid German radar, and bomb the MAN engine plant, a main producer of diesel engines for U-boats. Photographs and a scale model of the target area were provided. The aiming point was the manufacturing and assembly shops at the centre of the factory, a target just 600 by 300 feet.

The attack was to be carried out at less than 500 feet. Each Lancaster would carry four 500lb bombs with an 11-second delay fuse – to ensure that all aircraft crossed the target clear of the explosions. In the second section, Penman was in U-Uncle, Deverill his Number 2 in Y-Yorker, and Warrant Officer Mycock in P-Peter at No.3. They would be last over the target by which time the defences would be fully alerted.

Nuisance bombing raids with fighter support were being laid on to keep German fighters in northern France occupied, so the Lancaster force could slip by. Collier ended the briefing with: "I can't emphasise too strongly the importance of destroying this target. It's literally a matter of life and death in our struggle against the U-boats. That's all."

A pilot in the leading section, Flt Lt "Darkie" Hallows, recalled: "Plenty was said about how important it was and all that stuff, so we were obviously not intended to come back in any strength."

Take-off was at 3pm. One of the aircraft in the leading section had engine trouble starting up, so Rodley's aircraft took the No.2 place. The formation of seven (with the second reserve) flew down to the coast at Selsey Bill, where the reserve turned back.

At Selsey, the Lancs from Waddo came in sight but on a diverging course. Rodley said later: "We saw 44 Squadron slightly ahead of us, but realised they were drifting to port, and we continued in the direction we should have been going. Our six aircraft pressed on very, very low across the Channel so that we were underneath the radar." Sherwood and Penman maintained their compass heading as the 44 Squadron machines passed out of sight.

The formation crossed the Normandy coast at Dives-sur-Mer near Caen at about 16.45. They flew south-east, map-reading from one waypoint to the next. Timeless rural France flashed beneath their wings – farmhouses, fields, vineyards, villages, forests, rivers – as Sherwood's six aircraft swept very low over the countryside, rising and falling with the landscape.

Sgt Doug Overton, a gunner in Penman's aircraft, said later: "We kept low practically all the time – about 50 feet I should say. The front gunner was telling the pilot over the intercom about the high-tension cables. We were so low in places that I could see what colour ties and collars men were wearing."

Penman recalled: "It almost seemed, as we passed

over towns and villages, that we were flying between the clothes lines and chimney pots." At Sens, a key turning point, they swung east towards Bavaria. Approaching the German border, Penman lifted his three Lancasters over the green-wooded slopes of the Vosges mountains to cross the Rhine Valley near Basle, the peaks of the Alps rising tall on their right. "In France, people gave us the V-sign but in Germany they shook their fists at us", Overton said.

Skirting Switzerland and Lake Konstanz, they reached the last turning point, Ammersee, one of the large lakes dotting Bavaria – the nav. was "spot on". Here the three aircraft orbited briefly, to keep a safe interval from Sherwood's aircraft, somewhere ahead, since the target was now just 30 miles away. According to the timing, 44 Squadron must be well ahead out of sight.

The run in to Augsburg was over a rise approaching the city, which lay between wooded hills. Penman, with Mycock on his right, Deverill to his left, picked up a river leading to the factory. But the German defences were ready for them, firing from gunposts on the rooftops either side in a cross-barrage.

Rodley, ahead in the front section, recalled: "We were belting at full throttle at about 100 feet towards the target. I dropped the bombs along the side wall. We flashed across the target and down the other side to about 50 feet, because flak was quite heavy. As we went away I could see light flak shells overtaking us, green balls flowing away on our right and hitting the ground ahead of us."[78]

The defending gunners began scoring hits early on as the last three Lancasters made their run in, their gunners shooting back. Ron Irons: "The German defences were very alert and firing everything imaginable at us..." Mycock's P-Peter was soon set on fire as Penman led past tall factory chimneys. Ahead of them, smoke and flames could be seen erupting at the target.

All three were hit as they ran in: light flak, heavy flak, coloured tracer all coming at them. Mycock's port wing was burning fiercely and a fire grew inside the fuselage. A cannon shell punched through Deverill's wing, his starboard inner engine was set alight, a blaze started in the fuselage close to Mackay in the mid-upper turret.

"We're on fire", he called the pilot on the intercom. "Put it out then, I've got enough to do up here", came Deverill's answer. Irons and Mackay left their positions and tackled the blaze, from burning hydraulic oil, as Y-Yorker sped across the city, putting it out on the run in.

The factory roofs appeared in the bombsight from 400 feet and Y-Yorker's bombs went down. A brief view of "great big gaping holes", already blasted in the buildings, flashed by beneath.

All three aircraft had reached the target. But alongside Penman and Deverill, Mycock's P-Peter, which held formation until releasing its bombs, was finished. The crew of Y-Yorker saw it veer away and crash as the MAN plant receded behind.

Penman: "I increased power and dived as Deverill passed me with one engine feathered and the remaining three flat out. I called him and he asked me to cover his rear as his turrets were out of action. Ours had been unserviceable since the Channel, and as we had no wish to relinquish the navigation I told him to remain in position."

Penman and Deverill maintained formation then climbed to a safe height as it got dark, taking "a direct run home over Germany". Nearing the Channel coast, Deverill was able to restart the feathered engine.

Back in the Woodhall circuit, with the hydraulics damaged, he used the emergency system to lower the wheels and landed at 23.15. As Penman put it: "It says much for Deverill's skill that he remained in position until we reached the English coast and finally landed at Woodhall Spa." It had been an extraordinary day.

Debriefing and the next morning made the reckoning clear. Sherwood and Mycock had not come back. Rodley's words in the operational record explained, in brief: "Saw leader smoking and then a fire grew from his inner petrol tank and crash[ed] north of town in ball of flames."[79]

The four aircraft that got back were a sorry sight. Penman's U-Uncle had got away with holes from light flak, the others were seriously damaged. Deverill's aircraft showed a gaping gash under the starboard wing where the fuselage skin and part of the bomb bay floor burned through. Radio operator and gunner had put out the blaze with no time to spare.

As for 44 Squadron, the reports came that it had met disaster. Instead of a clear run across France, Nettleton's formation was attacked by German fighters soon after entering Normandy.

Their track took them alongside an aerodrome and in 15 minutes four of his six aircraft were shot down into the fields. Though Nettleton and his Number 2 reached the target, his was the only Lancaster of the six to return.

The newspapers splashed the raid on their front pages, with explanations on inside pages of how it was achieved. Winston Churchill, the Prime Minister, promptly sent a stirring message to Air Marshal Harris, saying:

We must plainly regard the attack of the Lancasters on the U-boats engine factory at Augsburg as an outstanding achievement of the

Docking vicarage, where Ernest applied for a special licence to marry
Joyce. The vicar met his parishioners in the study left of the front door

Below: The wedding party at North Farm, July 1940. Back row, left to
right: John Burgis, Jack Marshall (best man), Rita Burgis, Richard Burgis,
Doreen Deverill, Ernest Deverill snr. Front row, left to right: Elsie
Deverill, Ernest and Joyce, Blanche Burgis

Pilot Officer Deverill photographed for the notice board after he joined 97 Squadron at RAF Coningsby, September 1941

The troublesome Avro Manchester, which was grounded several times. An engine could break up without warning, making every sortie fraught with risk

Below: Officers, WAAFs and firing party at the funeral of Pilot Officer Hodge after the Dunkirk raid. Deverill is shown fourth from left

Above: 97 Squadron aircrews who returned from the Augsburg raid. F/O Deverill is sitting in front row, fourth from right. His crew are, back row: Sgt Irons (second from right); middle row: Sgt Devine, Sgt Mackay, Sgt Cooper, Flt Sgt Keane (fifth to eighth from left); front row: P/O Butler (on Deverill's left)

Left: Ernest and Joyce visit his parents at Dover in May 1942 while he was on special leave after the Augsburg attack

Left: Ernest, third from right, with his crew and Lancaster W-William (R5559), their regular aircraft at Woodhall Spa from mid-1942

Left: Lancasters over the target: the maelstrom of fires and flak bursts bomber crews saw as a raid developed

LANCASTER I.

Someday Peter, you'll be flying something even bigger & better than W-William

Left: Ernest's friendly note to Peter, son of the couple in Boston who welcomed the pilot into their home during his 97 Squadron tour

IWM

Above: Lancasters in loose formation speed low over the French countryside to attack the complex at Le Creusot, when Deverill's crew bombed at low level. Late afternoon shadows indicate the force is nearing its target

Below: Telegram from Flt Lt Hind, adjutant of 97 Squadron, congratulates Ernest on the Bar to his DFC

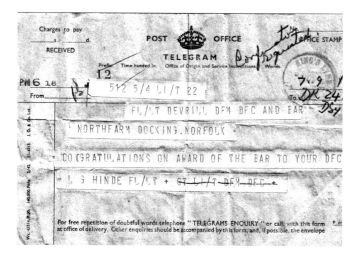

Above: Spitfires of the AFDU fighter affiliation 'circus', engine cowlings off for servicing, at a gloomy RAF Swinderby in December 1943. Flt Lt Deverill was flying these 'Spits' until November. The bombers are Short Stirlings of 1660 Heavy Conversion Unit where he crewed up to return to ops

Left: Though far from new the AFDU's Mark II Spitfires had ample performance for mock attacks

Left: Wartime crowds take a close look at P-Peter (R5552) displayed in Leeds city centre during Wings for Victory Week, June 1943. This aircraft was flown by Ernest Deverill the year before

Above: Air Vice-Marshal Don Bennett, straight-talking commander of the Pathfinder force where navigation was the name of the game.
Right: Wing Commander Hamish Mahaddie, Bennett's 'poacher' who sought out the best crews he could find for Pathfinders

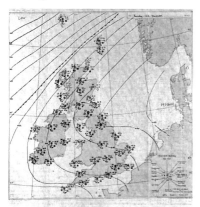

Left: Air Ministry summary chart for Thursday December 16 1943 showing high-pressure fog conditions over Britain. A weather front in the Atlantic moving eastwards will bring rain and milder weather in two days

Above: Entry in a 97 Squadron log on December 16. It shows the latitude and longitude positions given to navigators to plot their route to Berlin and back

Above: Joyce and her mother Blanche walk on
the promenade at Hunstanton after the war

Below: Main runway at the former RAF Woodhall Spa, from
which Ernest Deverill flew on many raids, is part of a
Lincolnshire nature reserve in the 21st century

**Royal Air Force. Undeterred by heavy losses
at the outset, 44 and 97 Squadrons pierced in
broad daylight into the heart of Germany and
struck a vital point with deadly precision.**

**Pray convey the thanks of His Majesty's
government to the officers and men who
accomplished this memorable feat of arms in
which no life was lost in vain.**

Later, Brendan Bracken, the government's Propaganda
Minister, held a press conference in London for news
reporters and the newsreel cameras, with some of the
Augsburg men present.

Ernest Deverill wasn't there, he was among those
sent on special leave. However, Ron Irons, the wireless
operator, was one of the small group of airmen looking
uncomfortable in front of the cameras.

Nettleton talked freely about the raid saying: "Even in
Germany people, especially children, waved to us, though
I doubt if they knew who we really were." Penman used
few words to tell of 97 Squadron's part in the operation:
"We had to do it. We did it. We got home. That's all there
is to it," he said.[80]

COUNTING THE COST

Public praise was followed by awards to 97 and 44 squadron airmen who had taken part. Ernest Deverill was among the officers of the two squadrons awarded the Distinguished Flying Cross, in the joint citation. There were DFMs for Ron Irons and Ken Mackay for putting out the fire and saving the aircraft. During his leave Dev and Joyce visited his parents at Dover.

The raid was a spectacular demonstration that the RAF had a capable new aircraft that could reach targets far into Germany. But the cost in men and machines could not be ignored. As Rodley recalled years later, the Augsburg raid was "a pretty hair-raising affair".

It can be said that Ernest Deverill's award was not entirely unexpected. Cuthbert Orde's joking comment to his fighter pilot sitter in 1941 ("The people I draw always seem to get the DFC"), had proved true for Ernest 12 weeks after his portrait was made.

Perhaps with the Augsburg raid in mind, another cautious memo was put out at Boscombe Down on April 24. It said: "I think we are reasonably safe in allowing the Command to continue flying the Lancaster, provided they maintain the daily inspection we have called for in the attached signal."

The Deverill crew's first op after returning from leave was a "gardening" trip in Z-Zebra (R5497) on the night of May 7/8. Four aircraft, each carrying six mines, were despatched to "sow" them in shipping lanes in the "Forget-me-not" code area, close to the naval port of Kiel, in the

Baltic Sea. The aim of the sortie was to disrupt use of the Kiel Canal, a vital 60-mile shortcut between the North Sea and the Baltic.

Mining sorties involved skilled navigation at night to make a timed run from a fixed land point, releasing the mines at two to three-second intervals. Further, the mines had to be dropped at low level.

In moonlight, Deverill dropped them in the right place from 700 feet, he reported at debriefing, but flak and machine-gun tracer from two small ships put a hole in the wing. This could be shrugged off, but it was a reminder that, even on a gardening trip, the risks should not be underestimated.

That Friday morning, Lord Trenchard himself, accompanied by Air Vice-Marshal Coryton, commander of 5 Group, visited Woodhall Spa "to interview the Augsburg raid aircrews", as the squadron log recorded.

Trenchard had not been idle since his official retirement in 1929. He was a controversial "new broom" during four years as head of the Metropolitan Police in London. Later, he got into prickly disputes when speaking up over the RAF's preparations for war.

Now in his late sixties and using a stick, the great man cast formality aside when visiting operational squadrons. He could charm the young airmen with his direct questions and self-deprecating stories, and by his appearance.

During one such visit, one of the airmen noticed that Trenchard's uniform with its four or five rows of medals "though absolutely immaculate, was obviously well-worn; and a cap, which apart from the badge, the 'scrambled egg' and its cleanliness, might easily have belonged to one of the squadron pilots".[81]

Trenchard's keenness to hear the personal experiences

of the Augsburg men can be in little doubt; he must have pressed them closely for their accounts.

That night, Deverill's crew were sent back to the Baltic, one of nine aircraft as part of a force briefed to bomb the Heinkel aircraft factory at Rostock. It was a difficult attack: dazzle from searchlights made it impossible to identify the target so they bombed by estimate.

As he reported at debriefing, the aircraft was "held in searchlights and subjected to intense, accurate heavy flak, also some light flak". All nine got back but 44 Squadron at Waddington had a disastrous night: four of its aircraft were missing.

Another mining trip to the Baltic, to the "Sweet pea" area near Rostock, followed mid-month. Deverill's was the sole aircraft on this "uneventful" trip, before a break of a few days.

For his next op, on the night of May 19/20, seven crews were briefed to attack Mannheim in south-west Germany. Deverill's aircraft, Z-Zebra again, left the runway at 22.31 and they climbed to form part of a mixed bag of almost 200 aircraft: twin-engine Hampdens, Wellingtons and Manchesters, four-engine Stirlings, Halifaxes and Lancasters. Whatever Bomber Command could throw at the city.

No sooner was Z-Zebra airborne than the intercom started to play up, interfering with communication between the crew. However they pressed on. The force flew south, passing over London. Meanwhile, far below in the leafy county of Surrey – unknown to the crews sitting at their aircraft positions – a remarkable event was unfolding.

Radio engineers from the BBC had arrived and set up recording equipment in the porch at the home of the celebrated cellist Beatrice Harrison. The engineers were there to make a live broadcast, as they did each spring. This was to bring to the nation the song of a nightingale in the woods as it responded to Harrison's music while she practised on her cello in the garden. This had been an annual event for almost 20 years, making the musician known across the world.

As the recording ran a nightingale began its song. But then, barely noticeable at first, a distant drone began to intrude. The noise grew into the deep growl of approaching aircraft, steadily increasing in volume.

Against this intrusion the nightingale continued to sing, its clear, liquid notes pitched above the vengeful roar of 500 aero engines. The noise of aircraft rose to a crescendo high overhead, then slowly faded into the distance as the bombers passed on.

The broadcast was quickly cut short for security reasons but, embedded within that sound of engines – recorded for posterity – were the four Merlins of Ernest Deverill's Lancaster. However, Z-Zebra did not get to Mannheim. By the time the French coast was reached, at 13,000 feet, the intercom had failed completely. There was no choice but to turn back.

THE 1,000 RAIDS

An exceptional number of aircraft movements at Lincolnshire aerodromes during the following week signalled that something very big was planned. Every aircraft that could carry bombs and be made available was arriving and being prepared.

Well-worn training aircraft, with their crews and instructors, were landing; and planes "borrowed" from Coastal Command. Deverill's old squadron of 206, now based in Northern Ireland, contributed 12 Hudsons. Their crews flew in to RAF North Coates on the Lincolnshire coast in readiness. Aircrews were confined to camp and slept in tents to maintain security. Thundery weather kept up the suspense.

Rumours spread as the week progressed. Behind the scenes, Air Marshal Harris wanted a largescale and spectacular success to prove that Bomber Command was essential to the war effort. Elements of a huge bombing armada had parked on dozens of stations in eastern England.

By Saturday May 30 the op was on. About 6,000 men packed into afternoon briefings at the stations. The atmosphere was expectant. The target was Cologne, Germany's third-largest city, with three aiming points. This would be the first raid carried out by 1,000 aircraft.

For the first time bombers would fly not in small numbers but one big stream, putting them across the target in as short a time as possible. The raid would last just 90 minutes. It could alter the course of the war, crews were told at the briefings.

Deverill's crew were one of 16 in the battle order at Woodhall Spa. The C.O, "Boy" Collier, was flying with them having put his name on the list. The ribbon on the briefing room wall map showed a straight in, straight out route across Holland except for a turn and short final leg, plus another after leaving the target.

Most of the force were also carrying incendiaries to set the city ablaze and overwhelm its fire services. However, 97 Squadron would be in the final group of 200 Halifaxes and Lancasters. They were timed to arrive in the last 15 minutes to drop 4,000lb high-explosive "blockbusters" plus incendiaries.

Crews were instructed to look for a place to bomb that was not already burning well. Bright full-moon conditions promised good visibility at the target, the met man said. That could be good hunting for German night fighters but, anticipating this, intruder aircraft were being sent to bomb the fighter airfields. This was a short trip of $3\frac{1}{2}$ to four hours. Flak and fighters were a certainty, but there was general relief that it was not a trip to the Ruhr.

Woodhall's Lancasters took off a few minutes after midnight. Deverill in W-William (R5559) was airborne at 00.11. One aircraft failed to get away because of a broken tailwheel, a second turned back with oil-pressure problems. The climb to operational height through thick thundery cloud brought a worrying risk of icing up, but conditions gradually improved over Europe. An orange glow could be seen ahead at a great distance. Unmistakably it was Cologne – well alight.

The squadron bombed from 15,000 feet-plus. Flying Officer Friend, the Rhodesian second pilot/navigator in M-Mother, observed: "As we crossed the town there were burning blocks to the right of us while to the left the fires were immense. Buildings were skeletons in the midst of fires... The blast of the bombs was hurling walls themselves across the flames."[82]

Yet 97 Squadron encountered few difficulties with flak and fighters. "Trip seemed to be an unqualified success", one crew reported at debriefing. When Deverill returned at 3.30am, the crew summed up for the record: "A very quiet trip, practically no opposition, only slight searchlight activity." Collier concluded his report with: "Trip amazingly uneventful." But for many inexperienced crews in obsolescent aircraft, it was a different story.

A second 1,000-strong attack was mounted for the night of June 1/2, with bomb loads the same. The target was factories at Essen. Deverill was in the battle order, but aircraft numbers were fewer this time. Cloud and the Ruhr's industrial haze proved a handicap which reduced the effects of the bombing. "Trip to and from the target much livelier than two nights ago,", one crew reported at debriefing. For Deverill the verdict was: "Average flak and searchlight activity over large area. Uneventful outward and return journey."

Over the next few days the Press and newsreels reported that the centre of Cologne was devastated. Remarkably, after the smoke cleared, daylight reconnaissance photos also showed that the soaring Gothic cathedral, while damaged, was intact.

The crew were on a run of good trips as raids on the Ruhr industrial cities plus "gardening" sorties resumed. Then a third "1,000 raid" was assembled, this time to Bremen, for the night of June 25/26. Again, Deverill's crew were listed to go. They had already attacked the city that month, on June 3/4, followed by two ops to Essen. For this huge effort against Bremen all 5 Group crews were briefed to bomb the Focke-Wulf aircraft factory. Squadrons in the other groups were to attack the shipyards, the town and the docks.

However, not long after Deverill took off, "gremlins" jammed one of the Lanc's main petrol cocks. Determined efforts to free it failed. So, with fuel supply to the engines compromised, they returned and were back on the runway after 45 minutes. In the next few days, they were sent to Bremen twice on much smaller raids, meeting "considerable flak over the target" in the first, the squadron losing an aircraft.

To mark these big attacks Air Marshal Harris, rarely seen at his bomber stations, gave an interview for Pathé News, filmed in his office for the nation's cinema audiences. Looking directly at camera over his reading glasses Harris gave a warning:

Cologne, Lubeck, Rostock, they are just the beginning. We cannot send 1,000 bombers a time over Germany every time as yet but the time will come when we can do so... It may take a year, it may take two, but for the Nazis the writing is on the wall... There are a lot of people who say that bombing can never win a war. Well, my answer to that is it has never been tried yet and we shall see.

RAF wives such as Joyce, who lived at home far from the stations, found ways to manage the periods of separation until their husband's next leave. Bomber crews were granted a week's leave every six weeks, though this could be "mucked up" at short notice by operational demands.

Many women created an independent life when their

husband was not there, carrying out the responsibilities if they had children. Joyce was still employed in her war work at the Food Office, and leader of Docking Guides. Unlike wives who stayed in "digs" or perhaps a room over a pub near the aerodrome, she provided a home life at the farmhouse for Dev when his leave permitted.

Large numbers of women were at work for the first time, finding opportunities and earning their own money as they responded to a national call to back the war effort. Women aged 18 to 60 had been required to register for war work since early 1941. Conscription for single women aged 20-30 followed in December. Those not doing war work were given a choice: take employment in industry, such as the aircraft factories, or join one of the auxiliary services.

These services were civil defence, the ATS (Auxiliary Territorial Service), the WAAF (Women's Auxiliary Air Force), and the WRNS (Women's Royal Naval Service). Thousands were in the Women's Voluntary Service (WVS), assisting in hospitals, running emergency rest centres, and the familiar mobile canteens serving tea and buns to rescue workers and service personnel.

Volunteers in the Women's Land Army were working up to 50 hours a week in place of men on farms to increase food production, and in forests to boost timber supplies. "Land girls", many from big cities, were trained for tasks ranging from dairy work – milking cows, making cheese and butter – to labour in the fields, working with horse teams, driving tractors, and bringing in the harvest.

Off-duty, Ernest Deverill was one of many RAF men away from home to be befriended by Lincolnshire families. He got to know a business couple living in Boston, 15 miles from Woodhall. They were Alf and Flo Reynolds who ran Reynolds & Son, the town's main grocer and wine merchant. Ernest became a regular visitor to their home. The eldest of their two sons, Peter, aged about eight, looked up to "Uncle Dev". He, in turn, encouraged Peter's interest in flying. Ernest's cheery note of support, written under a picture of a Lancaster, captures the friendship between them.

After Peter started at Ratcliffe College, a boarding school near Leicester, Ernest's crew "made a noisy low-level visit in their Lancaster". The college was set in extensive grounds and, an account says, "they roared in one day to buzz the place, dropping sweets for the pupils. Sweets were in short supply in the school because of the war".

By late-June 1942 the Deverill crew were flying regularly in W-William (R5559); and Ernest had a new gunner, Jim Benbow. In 1940, Benbow, in his early thirties, had left a settled life in Middlesbrough running a cafe business with his wife Madge to volunteer for the RAF. He soon was a regular in the rear turret.

That month, the squadron was notified via the Red Cross that Squadron Leader Sherwood was alive and a prisoner of war. It was barely believable in view of the fact his aircraft was observed to crash in flames at Augsburg. The rest of the crew apparently had not survived. It remained to be seen how Sherwood could have escaped certain death.

A few weeks later a postcard arrived addressed to Flight Lieutenant Hind, the squadron adjutant. The card was from Sherwood, posted from a German prisoner-of-war camp and dated June 26. It began: "Dear Hind, just a line to let you and the boys know I am ok. I got away with a burnt face followed by scarlet fever. I have no news of the rest of the crew and fear the worst..."[83]

On the night of August 28/29 Deverill's luck held again, just, during a raid on Nuremburg. This was a long haul to southern Germany. Visibility was good when the 97 Squadron Lancasters arrived so the target was not difficult to identify: the city was already burning from the initial attack by Pathfinders.

Deverill in N-Nuts bombed from 13,000 feet. But, in a reminder of the Dunkirk attack nine months before, a flak burst smashed one of the cockpit observation blisters. This time there were no serious consequences. For the squadron record they summed up their sortie as "A successful trip", which was the general view at debriefing. However, one aircraft did not return.

The repair system for damage from enemy action involved a small team of Avro engineers on the station who made an assessment and carried out the work if it could be done at the airfield. Aircraft requiring a lot of work were transported to Avro's centralised repair works near Lincoln.

If not written off, a badly damaged machine was taken back to the factory in sections to be rebuilt. An engineer at another bomber station, asked to examine a Lancaster at dispersal, recalled:

As it had been on a bombing raid over Germany the previous night everything was in place – the ammunition racks leading to the gun positions were full of live bullets, all of different colours denoting their particular use.

One in every ten was a tracer – then came incendiaries, armour piercing and, to make up the ten, the ordinary bullet. On entering the aircraft, I could feel the atmosphere – the smell of sweating bodies, disinfectant from the Elsan, gunpowder and stale breath. The interior was still warm from the previous night's operation.[84]

Deverill's crew had a run of fairly easy, even routine, ops in early September, to targets that included Saarbrucken, Karlsruhe and Bremen. They were not much troubled by the opposition though one crew failed to return from Saarbrucken and another did not get back from Bremen.

Mid-month, exceptionally, Deverill flew as captain with a different crew, perhaps replacing a pilot who was sick. The target was the docks at Wilhelmshaven, on Germany's North Sea coast, which they bombed from 16,000 feet. An "uneventful trip", they reported at debriefing.

The regular crew were listed only once more that month, for a trip to Munich. But they had to turn back "owing to loss of oil and petrol". Then in the last week a number of ops were cancelled because of bad weather.

Mid-month, Air Marshal Harris sent one of his cheerleading signals to all 5 Group squadrons. It read: "Would you please convey to all aircrews and ground personnel that their recent efforts have achieved most outstanding success and that the squadrons have now become almost a byword in the whole command.

"There is no doubt that the country as a whole, and the Air Force in particular, owe them the greatest thanks. Winston's famous saying after the Battle of Britain undoubtedly is also applicable to your squadrons."

LOW-LEVEL AGAIN

Mid-October 1942 brought a raid that demonstrated the RAF's power to hit an important target in force using the increasing number of Lancasters available. Again, some 97 Squadron crews were chosen for special training, Deverill's being among them.

Lancasters from all nine squadrons of 5 Group were sent out to practise formation flying across eastern England. As in the days before the Augsburg raid in April, it was quickly realised that something "big" was on.

Briefing was on the morning of Saturday October 17th. Nine 97 Squadron crews were called. The curtain was pulled back to reveal the target. This was a daylight raid on the Schneider works, a huge armaments and locomotive manufacturing plant at Le Creusot in eastern France, which was supplying the German war effort.

Crews were told that bombing accuracy was essential because many workers' homes were adjacent to the "vast area of factories, workshops and warehouses".

It was a combined daylight operation led by Wing Commander Leonard "Slosher" Slee of 49 Squadron, timed to arrive at the target at dusk. Responsibility for getting the force there on time rested with Slee's Australian navigator, Flying Officer Arthur Grant.

To help navigators keep to timetable they were issued with specially prepared route maps giving the track from the French coast to Le Creusot. These were marked with waypoints that showed the distance remaining to the target. Reconnaissance photographs and information sheets were handed out, since the planning was as meticulous as possible.

Deverill's crew, in T-Tommy (W4278), were one of two from 97 Squadron briefed for a particular task. Six aircraft, led by Wing Commander Gibson of 106 Squadron, would split off to attack the electrical transformer and switching station at Montchanin, five miles from Le Creusot. This installation supplied the manufacturing complex with its power and wrecking it would by itself stop production. The load for this was eight 500lb bombs, to be dropped at low level, aiming at the main control room.

The nine Lancasters took off from Woodhall at midday and set course south-west through the Midlands. Near Swindon they and other formations joined up with Slee, creating a force that totalled 94 Lancasters.

The formation sped across Devon to leave the coast at Start Point, the roar of more than 370 Merlins spreading over the countryside. They were already flying low, three groups stepped at 800, 600 and 400 feet to keep under the cloud base of only 1,000 feet. Over the sea they settled at about 300 feet in loose formation for the long crossing over the Bay of Biscay to western France.

By now the weather had improved, with bright sunshine and crews relaxing in shirtsleeves. The French coast was crossed south of the six miles-long Isle d'Yeu, a coastal island south-west of Nantes – Grant's navigation was spot on. Slee took the Lancasters down to less than 100 feet and "the formation flew the whole way between heights of 50 and 500 feet", roaring eastwards over the sunbathed countryside.[85]

A sergeant pilot said: "We hedge-hopped across France. It was like a Grand National Steeplechase. Some French waved, others did not seem to notice us. Cows, chickens, horses and dogs bolted as we roared over their heads. A duck came through the windscreen and the gun turret was full of feathers."[86]

A few aircraft had to return early while the rest pressed on to the last waypoint, the town of Nevers. It was easy to recognise on a loop of the River Loire, leaving about 60 miles to the target. At the front, green Very lights shot out from Slee's aircraft, signalling the main force to begin the climb for their bombing run.

It was now near 6pm, with dusk approaching. Gibson's six Lancasters with Deverill's T-Tommy separated to the right and stayed low heading to Montchanin. They identified the transformer station by its proximity to small lakes near the town.

The six attacked in turns at just 500 feet, at intervals to reduce the risk to their aircraft from the explosions. Then the attackers circled the plant, gunners firing at the transformers standing in the open, which sparked brilliant-blue flashes as hits registered. However, one aircraft was in trouble during the attack and seen to crash some distance away. Only five aircraft set course for home. Meanwhile, Le Creusot was covered with a pall of smoke rising from the main attack. It had lasted just seven minutes.

The weather was poor again on their return and half the aircraft were diverted to airfields in the south of England. T-Tommy landed at 10.22pm, Deverill's crew having been up for more than ten hours. His summary of the raid at debriefing for the squadron record was precise and technical, from his electrical training:

Bombs seen to overshoot main control room but to straddle isolating switch house and 120KW transformers. Whole area inside wire fence machine gunned.

The next day brought high praise for the crews in a signal from Harris. His message to 5 Group read:

Congratulations to all concerned in yesterday's brilliantly executed and highly successful operation... The timing and navigation to within one minute and less than one mile over 2,000 miles, and the landing of nearly 100 aircraft in darkness under bad weather conditions on strange bases without bending a rivet, evidence a standard of airmanship throughout your Command which has yet to be surpassed.

However, airmen in the main attack had watched in dismay as their bombs fell on to homes as well as the factory complex. Later, British newspapers quoted brief French reports, one stating: "Vichy radio says total number killed in the raid has risen to 57. Sixty houses were destroyed and 300 were damaged." According to one senior RAF commander, writing later, Harris was disappointed to learn that the attack was not accurate enough.

At 97 Squadron, some relief came in the debriefing report from Wing Commander Jones's crew. It ended with: "Judging by the number of people who waved to us and the number of lights flashed from houses after dusk, there is nothing wrong with the spirit of France."

The missing aircraft, from 61 Squadron, was believed to have struck a building at Montchanin before crashing.[87] But a brief note Deverill wrote next to his logbook entry suggests more than that. The note says: "Damaged by own bombs."

His aircraft was not the only one. The morning after the raid Flt Lt Hopwood of 106 Squadron, who took part in the attack on the transformer station, made a phone call to his flight commander, Sqn Ldr John Searby. Calling from an airfield near Oxford, Hopwood asked if he could have a lift back to Syerston. The reason, he said casually, was his Lanc "needs a patch here and there".

Searby flew down in a spare aircraft. He found: "Hoppy's Lancaster was a mess; the blast from his five 1,000-pound bombs had wiped off the bomb bay doors and torn the bottom out of the fuselage in various places... One engine nacelle lacked its rear portion and the tailplane assembly had more holes than metal... Yet he had made a perfect landing on the last pint of fuel from his damaged tanks."[88]

There was little respite after the Le Creusot raid. A formation flying exercise ordered on October 20 made clear that again something intriguing was planned. On the 22nd, nine crews including Deverill's were called to a briefing for a long-distance trip to bomb Genoa, the Italian port squeezed between mountains and the Mediterranean Sea. Bomber Command was sending about 100 Lancasters led by Pathfinders to disrupt Axis supplies by sea from Italy to north Africa. This attack was to aid the British Eighth Army fighting in the Western Desert.

Deverill, taking a second pilot, flew a different aircraft to his usual W-William. This was a long trip carrying bombs and incendiaries, so requiring full tanks. Take-off was at dusk soon after 5pm. The formation flew south-east across France in clear weather under an almost full moon. In its light they crossed the majestic Alps, which by one description stood "glistening white and almost purple in the shadows".

There was cloud over the target, but the Pathfinder aircraft dropped flares as markers in the bright moonlight.

Deverill bombed visually from 10,000 feet, reporting later: "... Attack appeared to be well concentrated. Good fires burning and were visible 100 miles away".

Poor weather at base on the return forced a diversion to Stradishall, in Suffolk, where they touched down at 02:20. They had been in the air for just over nine hours. "Perfect air raid", Deverill noted in his logbook.

On October 24, the battle order showed another op to Italy and, like Le Creusot, this was a daylight trip. The target was Milan, the city's rail marshalling yards the aiming point. This time Deverill's crew were one of seven put up by 97 Squadron.

Take-off was shortly after noon. To avoid attention over France, the almost 90 Lancasters made their own way to rendezvous over Lake Annecy in the French Alps, three hours' flying. They then crossed into Italy.

Arriving on time, the force bombed through gaps in the 8/10ths cloud that covered Milan. The raid lasted 18 minutes, starting many large fires, with little flak from half-hearted defences. The aircraft returned across France in darkness. Bad weather over Lincolnshire forced the 97 Squadron planes to be diverted, returning to base the next day. It was Deverill's second nine-hour trip in three days.

And that was it. His tour was over. The crew were "screened" to be rested, split up, and some posted. Jim Benbow and Ron Irons stayed on for a second tour.

Ernest Deverill had flown 40 operations in an extraordinary year. He was at the centre of events in Bomber Command's growing ability to carry the war into Europe.

He also had gained two promotions during his time with the Squadron, from Pilot Officer to Flying Officer, then Flight Lieutenant. On November 1, Sqn Ldr Coton, commander of B Flight, signed the logbook and Ernest went on 10 days' leave before taking up his new posting.

At North Farm, a telegram arrived from Flt Lt Hind, the squadron adjutant, offering his congratulations on the award of a Bar to his DFC. As a local paper, the *Lynn Advertiser*, put it soon after: "A London daily says, "They call him 'The Devil' at his bomber station, because of his utter contempt for enemy fighters and ack-ack opposition."

The DFC was a "gong" commonly awarded to officers at the end of their tour. This could give rise to good-humoured mockery in the mess as it was not "earned" for any one action, but the citation was clear enough:

> **Since being awarded the DFC this officer has taken part in 30 sorties, including many attacks on targets in the Ruhr area. In the daylight attack on the transformer station near Le Creusot Flight Lieutenant Deverill bombed his objective from a height of 500 feet.**
>
> **He also participated in the recent raids on Milan and Genoa. This officer has invariably endeavoured to press home his attacks with great vigour.**

Put another way, Ernest Deverill earned the Bar for surviving against the odds.

SOME KIND OF REST

Flight Lieutenant Deverill was posted on November 11 1942 to the Air Fighting Development Unit (AFDU) at RAF Duxford, near Cambridge. Duxford, like Bircham Newton, dated from the last war. In contrast to the neatly laid-out Norfolk station, it was a jumbled accumulation of buildings, Nissen huts and air-raid shelters.

The AFDU was no ordinary posting. This was a high-powered specialist unit that advised on technical intelligence to the RAF and Air Ministry. It had an establishment at the time of about 160 officers, airmen, WAAFs and civilians.

Its work included flying trials to assess new/modified Allied aircraft and equipment. Captured German aircraft were flown to assess their performance. Frequent visits by RAF top brass, Air Ministry specialists, plus visits to factories such as Rolls-Royce, meant plenty of comings and goings.

The unit was headed by Wing Commander Ian Campbell-Orde. In July that year he had carried out full performance trials of the first Focke-Wulf 190 fighter to fall intact into Allied hands. This prize came about through an embarrassing mistake by the German pilot.

Disoriented after a combat over Devon, he flew *north* for "home"; and having crossed the Bristol Channel instead of the English Channel, believed he was in France. He landed at RAF Pembrey, a training station in south Wales, taxied in, only to be greeted by an alert duty pilot who quickly put him under arrest.

The FW190 had outclassed the Spitfire Mark V in air battles over northern France; the RAF had been desperate to get their hands on one to find out why. Among its novel features, it was found that the German aircraft had an advanced mechanical computer to control the engine, which reduced the pilot's workload during combat.

Deverill's new job was far from run of the mill for a pilot rested from operations. It was to set up and command a "fighter affiliation circus" – one of six units under the formal title of Demonstration Squadron. These were to be sent shortly on attachment, each to a different RAF Group.

Fighter affiliation, using a mix of ground instruction and mock combat exercises with bomber crews in the air, was designed to teach aircrews effective defensive tactics to use when they encountered enemy fighters. The aim was to reduce losses on operations. Deverill's "circus" would be attached to 5 Group at RAF Swinderby, near Lincoln. His technical abilities and recent operational experience on four-engine "heavies" made him well qualified for this work. Fighter pilots posted to AFDU usually were not experienced on multi-engine aircraft.

The AFDU carried out affiliation exercises with hand-me-down Mk11 Spitfires from a maintenance unit, flown as "enemy aircraft". Ernest Deverill took up a "Spit" for the first time on November 16, for 15 minutes. Next day he went up for a 20-minute air test, then for half an hour of aerobatics to get his hand in. So he became a Spitfire pilot, with a licence to enjoy the sheer exhilaration of flying this thrilling aircraft. And he was ready to give bomber crews some awkward surprises.

He set up base at Swinderby with three Spitfires and a small team of fitters to maintain them. Swinderby was a busy training station where a number of different units were based, a place increasingly crowded with personnel.

The aerodrome sprawled beside the main road that ran between Lincoln and Newark-on-Trent. As a wartime bomber base it had the usual three concrete runways laid in triangular pattern. The main runway was parallel to the road, the arrow-straight Roman route Fosse Way. Pilots landing in poor visibility risked landing on the road accidentally, which was not unknown. In one episode it resulted in a heated argument there and then between the pilot and his commander.

The affiliation schedule required Deverill to manage a schedule and fly out in a Spitfire to 5 Group squadrons, at Waddington, Syerston, Fulbeck, Bottesford, Langar and elsewhere, for the exercises and analysis. These affiliation flights lasted between 30 minutes and $1\frac{1}{2}$ hours. Bombers would climb to operational height, then radio for the fighter to come up.

Pilot Officer Leonard Thorne, long-serving at ADFU, recalled from his own experience: "Usually not more than four bombers would take part in each sortie, taking it in turns to be the target aircraft. The fighter would carry out mock attacks on each in turn. In this way, most of the bomber crews got their chance to practise taking evasive action, particularly by 'corkscrewing'."[89]

A Lancaster navigator explained: "We were taught, if you're being attacked by a fighter, it's obviously going to come in tail-end either from your port or starboard stern. The first thing you do when you see this fighter coming in is start a 'corkscrew' in that direction. This is where the air-gunners come into their own.

"The air-gunner, tail or mid-upper, will call out 'Fighter, fighter! Port stern, corkscrew port'. That told us we'd got a fighter coming on from the port side, now we are going to meet it; and that will shorten the distance between the two aeroplanes to a considerable extent and shorten his aim and more or less put him on his nose."

These exercises were no polite demonstration. The task of the Spitfire pilot was to use his skills and the element of surprise to simulate a real attack. Alerted by his gunners, the bomber pilot wrenched his controls full over, throwing the aircraft into a steep diving turn, then reversing them to pull up again in a steep climb.

"Quite frankly", the navigator said, "you can turn a fighter over on its back because of the disturbance of the air and he can drop some thousands of feet before he makes any sort of recovery. During one of these exercises we went down like a bomb and the fighter got in so close I could almost see the colour of his eyes."[90]

Wing Commander John Searby, made C.O. of 83 Squadron in the Pathfinder Force, wrote after the war: "There was no formula for survival in a bomber aircraft at night over enemy occupied territory save that of constant vigilance. The interval between observing the enemy and taking evasive action was of the order of two or three seconds only, and less if possible. Instant reaction to the warning cry from the watching gunners was essential."[91]

By 1943, airmen flying in Bomber Command, in increasing numbers, were a huge mix from many countries: Australians, New Zealanders, Dutch, French, Polish, South Africans, Americans, Canadians, and from the Caribbean. Training for pilots and navigators came under the Commonwealth Air Training Plan carried out abroad, in America, Canada and elsewhere.

Most men were volunteers for a standard tour of 30

ops. As such they were a different breed from the regular servicemen like Ernest Deverill with years of experience.

The AFDU's affiliation units were teaching tried-and-tested methods to pass on hard-earned experience, yet some squadron commanders were against these tactics. They insisted bomber pilots should fly straight and level all the way to the target. This could stir an argument in the mess, with an outspoken junior officer at risk of being accused of insubordination. Yet German flak and fighter fire could not discriminate in favour of those "doing the right thing".

February 1943 was a significant month for Flt Lt Deverill. During the first week an official letter came from St James's Palace in London notifying him: "The King will hold an Investiture at Buckingham Palace on Tuesday, February 16 1943 at which your attendance is requested." This was to be presented with the Bar to his DFC.

The letter specified: "Dress – Service Dress, Morning Dress or Civil Defence Uniform". Two tickets were offered for relatives or friends to witness the ceremony. Joyce and Ernest's mother Elsie accompanied him as his guests to share the proud moment.

"These wartime investitures were comparatively simple ceremonies with a sombre dignity," recalled a senior WAAF who attended a number of them. "The King stood facing the assembled company... those receiving decorations walked in turn along the narrow platform past the King".

Afterwards, many of those attending had their photo taken in the crowd outside the palace gates, though no picture of the family there that day is known.

About this time, Ernest was sent back to Waddington for a Beam Approach refresher course with the BAT Flight, to maintain his skills landing in fog. Refreshers kept pilots up to date but it was still an "exercise"; that is, flying the beam under controlled conditions. It was an insurance policy yet to be called upon returning from an op.

Swinderby was a good distance from home in north Norfolk, though only 60 miles direct across the waters and sandbanks of The Wash. This was a short hop for a Spitfire and, on March 11, Ernest flew one to Docking. It must be that he "borrowed" the Spit to make the most of his leave with Joyce, parking the fighter at the aerodrome for some days.

RAF Docking, always a windy, inhospitable place, was a lot busier than it had been in 1940, with specialist units coming and going. Its grass runways also offered a welcome emergency landing ground for bomber crews returning from Europe.

In April, the AFDU moved base from Duxford to RAF Wittering in Cambridgeshire. Deverill's small team continued at Swinderby, where it had been since February. Leonard Thorne recalled: "It may seem that on these fighter affiliation trips we had long spells just sitting around doing nothing. This was not the case; I do not remember ever being bored. We were allowed to attend the briefings for the bomber crews and would later watch them taking off, fully loaded with petrol, bombs and ammunition.

"Some mornings we would get up very early to watch the survivors coming home. Later, we sometimes attended the de-briefings by the intelligence officers, and talked to the very tired crews. On days when there were no operations we could visit local places of interest. When at Waddington or Scampton, Lincoln was always a popular spot."

Constant contact with the officers and men of 5 Group will have kept Ernest Deverill well supplied with "pukka gen" about its successes and failures, in particular raids against cities in the Ruhr.

The "Battle of the Ruhr", between March and July 1943, was led by Pathfinder aircraft equipped with Oboe target-marking, a system using pulses sent from two ground stations in England. The campaign included two landmark raids in March against Essen, each carried out by more than 400 aircraft. Duisburg was severely damaged on May 12/13.

On the night of May 23/24 a force of 800-plus aircraft was sent to Dortmund and destroyed large areas of the city, helped by accurate marking in clear conditions. But Harris's campaign against Germany's industrial centres came at a high cost. The Ruhr was very well defended by fighters and flak batteries: as the raids got bigger bomber losses rose.

An attack by more than 700 aircraft on Wuppertal-Barmen, on the night of May 29/30, marked a turning point in the scale of destruction Bomber Command could inflict in a single raid. The city of Wuppertal, extending along the Wupper valley between steep hills, was known for its *Schwebebahn* public transport system, a "Meccano set" suspended railway that wound its way for 13-kilometres above the streets and river.

The RAF's target, on a Saturday night, was the town of Barmen, at the eastern end of the line, and birthplace of the philosopher Friedrich Engels. Barmen had factories and barracks but was only lightly defended. At briefing, one airman recalled, it was explained that it was a dormitory town for workers at the factories in Essen.

Visibility over the target was good and the marking by Pathfinder Mosquitoes (dropping cascading white "Christmas trees", as the Germans called them) was accurate. So was the bombing of this confined area from 18-20,000 feet.

Reports from crews in debriefing rated the operation a clear success, the defences "very poor". However, their descriptions to the intelligence officers revealed something more. From four crews of 97 Squadron:

Many big fires raging, well grouped round marked area.
Mass of fires seen with smoke up to 10,000 feet.
Whole town appeared to be circled in red fires.
Great columns of smoke over target area. One colossal fire seemed to spread over whole of target.

This last extract confirmed that flames and heat from the highly concentrated attack had merged into one big conflagration. Barmen was engulfed by a firestorm.

By a twist of Fate a young Englishwoman, Sybil Bannister, was staying in the town on a rare visit to her German in-laws. Her experience that night, recalled in harrowing detail, made her an extraordinary witness to the effect of the RAF's "area bombing".

THROUGH THE FLAMES

Sybil Bannister, a fluent German-speaker divorced from a German doctor, had travelled more than 600 miles to visit Barmen with her son Manny, aged two. They were staying at her father-in-law's home. Saturday May 29 was her birthday, with the afternoon spent at the house celebrating. They had coffee and cake with two other young mothers. That evening they shared a bottle of wine.

When the air raid siren sounded at about 1am and bombs began to fall she collected Manny from the top floor and rushed to the cellar with the others. As they reached it there was "a terrific explosion, followed by one after another".

The cellar filled with people seeking refuge, using torches because the power had cut. "Many arrived in their nightclothes. They came in with fractured limbs, streaming with blood, some of them badly burnt... And all the time the bombs were whistling down. Our lungs felt as though they would burst. We could not hear each other speak for the deafening explosions."

The stairs caught fire and a warden urged them to go to a municipal shelter nearby. Holding the child, Sybil Bannister squeezed through a gap into the next-door cellar, up to the entrance hall "flaring up like a matchbox".

She wrapped Manny in a thick rug and carried him into the street. It was full of smoke. "I tried to walk in the middle of the road because tongues of flame were leaping from every window and the trees at the edge of the pavement were also on fire, shedding blazing branches…

By that time the tar had melted and was burning." Burning houses had fallen into the road "then another collapsed in front of me – I was trapped."

"I chose the spot where the flames were only about knee-deep and made a dash for it… but gradually I was overcome by an appalling fatigue. When I dropped Manny into the flames he screamed and I picked him up again… it urged me to one more superhuman effort."

A rider on a motorcycle and sidecar stopped and took them to the town hall. Its cellar was full, "everyone as black as chimney sweeps". Mother and child were put on a lorry that took them high above the town to a school being used as a medical centre.

Their burns, caused by phosphorous medical helpers said, were treated in the cellar but the building was already alight and had to be evacuated. Bannister ran out with the boy as masonry crashed down. The firestorm was raging in the town below.

Next morning burnt bodies lay in the street. She reached a relative's house, where "she wept to see the sad spectacle we presented, covered in sooty grime, our eyelids swollen and red, burns on our hands and faces besides our bandaged legs, but above all the horrors of the night reflected in our eyes.

"Later we were told that many people with clothes on fire had jumped into the river and those who could not swim drowned. News of the disaster in Barmen spread like wildfire throughout Germany."[92]

The AFDU had various aircraft on its books including for testing, as communications hacks for local flights and to ferry personnel. Ernest Deverill's logbook shows he flew a number of them. AFDU pilots were expected to simply get in an unfamiliar machine and fly it. The hacks included a four-seat Stinson Reliant and Miles Magister, a monoplane trainer with open cockpits and fixed undercarriage. The Magister, unlike a Tiger Moth, had flaps and wheel brakes. On June 15 he flew the "Maggie" to Docking, returning the same day.

Test aircraft he flew included the powerful Douglas Boston bomber and twin-engine de Havilland Mosquito, the 400mph plywood and balsa fighter/bomber. The AFDU had the "Mossie" to carry out fuel consumption tests and Deverill flew it once, on June 28, taking it up for an affiliation with a Vickers Wellington. This in itself was exceptional flying since the Mossie was reckoned to be a "young man's machine" and not easily mastered.

Just a month later the Mosquito crashed spectacularly in the hands of another pilot while making an emergency landing. One engine had cut, forcing a landing, but the second engine stopped on final approach as the pilot opened up to avoid some airmen on bicycles. Leonard Thorne was sitting next to him in the navigator's seat. He recalled:

As we careered across the grass we shed first both engines, then the rear fuselage, and finally both wings… To the surprise of the crash wagon crew we stepped out of the wreck with only a few bumps and bruises.

It was another demonstration of the importance of luck in wartime flying.

On August 25, Deverill flew the Maggie to "Docking and return", evidently for a few days' leave as his next affiliation flight was on the 29th. However, his arrivals and departures at North Farm underlined the limited time he and Joyce had as a married couple.

Publicity from daring attacks such as the Augsburg raid and the "Dambusters" raid on the Ruhr dams in May 1943 had helped make the RAF increasingly familiar to the public. So had the sheer numbers of RAF and WAAF personnel in uniform to be seen in everyday life – at railway stations with their kitbags, at dances, in cinemas and in village pubs. This, and announcements of bravery awards for airmen, had brought the service the recognition it wanted.

However, it was a play on the London stage, *Flare Path* by Terence Rattigan, a serving RAF officer, which revealed the personal pressures bomber aircrew and women in their lives were under. Terence Rattigan had made his name as a playwright before the war with the West End comedy *French Without Tears*. *Flare Path* opened at the Apollo Theatre, Shaftesbury Avenue, on August 13 1942 after a four-week tour.

The first night was attended by the RAF's "top brass", with Air Chief Marshal Portal among them. Rattigan attended in uniform and recalled "spending most of that evening standing rigidly to attention, while Air Marshal after Air Marshal approached the humble Flying Officer to tell him how his play should really have been written."[93] Later, Winston Churchill himself went to see it. A year on, *Flare Path*, a popular success, was still running.

During late August and early September 1943 Bomber Command carried out a series of raids on Berlin. The German capital was a formidable target 600 miles distant, four hours' flying from the airfields of eastern England. Aircraft losses were large, especially of the more vulnerable Halifaxes and Stirlings which could not fly as high as the Lancasters. And the Lancaster was proving to have a lower loss rate.

Radar-equipped night fighters defended the skies over Holland and into Germany, while the large area of flak defences around Berlin took bombers about 25 minutes to fly through. In the city centre three concrete flak towers 130 feet high were equipped with heavy and light-calibre guns blazing shells up into the bomber stream.

To visit the operational stations where aircraft were returning shot-up or "failed to return", as AFDU pilots in an affiliation circus did, was an everyday acknowledgement of the odds bomber crews could not avoid.

The Australian pilot "Micky" Martin, who survived the war, saw this as "a total acceptance" of fate. "Either you were going to get through or you weren't and the mathematical chances of getting through the war were very long odds indeed. So therefore I never saved a penny. I spent everything that was ever sent to me."[94]

This was something the RAF did not want aircrews to think about. A statistician carrying out research for Bomber Command observed: "The whole weight of Air Force tradition and authority was designed to discourage the individual airman from figuring the odds."[95]

From the sorties of 1942 which relied on GEE and Oboe as bombing and navigation aids, bomber operations had developed into an electronic cat-and-mouse game in competition with the German defences. Both sides were testing and deploying measures and counter-measures to try to gain advantage.

However, at bomber stations in 1943 there was evidence of a breakthrough in target finding. A bulging Perspex cupola seen under the rear fuselage of the "heavies" indicated an aircraft that could "see through the clouds".

H2S was a secret ground-mapping radar devised by government "boffins" (physicists and inventors). Bombing blind from above cloud and beyond the range of Oboe was now a reality.

It was a complex item of equipment. Inside the cupola was mounted a three-foot-wide scanner and a high-power transmitter/receiver. With the scanner rotating beneath the aircraft at height, the transmitter pulsed high-frequency radio waves on the 10-centimetre wavelength to the ground below. The return signals were fed to a CRT (cathode ray tube) screen on the navigator's desk, displaying a moving image of the main ground features.

Generating the pulses was the unit's most secret component, the cavity magnetron, a small copper oscillator. H2S brought a considerable advance in bombing accuracy as well as a useful aid for navigators to fix an aircraft's position without relying solely on dead reckoning. So far as was known, the Germans did not have such a device. For this reason H2S was referred to in code – in squadron logs and debriefing reports – as "Y" or "special equipment".

H2S was in factory production as Bomber Command pushed to install the equipment in all its "heavies". But 10cm H2S badly needed improvement. Images on the CRT display were blurry, so navigators had to be carefully trained to interpret them correctly. The display also had temperamental "gaps and fades". When an aircraft rolled, the ground image tipped off the screen, a distracting problem during the bombing run.

The Y equipment produced best results when an aircraft passed above distinctive ground features such as coastline and large rivers. This had produced accurate target marking in the attacks in July on Hamburg, Germany's biggest port and second-largest city. The intense firestorm that resulted devastated a large area. Berlin though was more spread out and provided fewer features that H2S could show clearly. "The Big City", as aircrews called the capital, remained a tough proposition.

More was being done to protect the vulnerable bombers. In August 1943, 100 Group was formed with a plan to send radar-equipped intruder aircraft into Europe, flying with the bomber stream to pursue German night fighters. But by October the first squadrons could manage little more than training sorties. The twin-engine Beaufighters and well-worn Mosquitoes that 100 Group was allocated were inadequate. And worse, their AI (air interception) radar sets were unreliable.

By late autumn bad weather was another factor to be reckoned with. The Short Stirlings were withdrawn from Berlin operations because the risk to them of icing up in cloud was too high. In the last week of October all ops and flying training were cancelled because of heavy rain, mist and fogs.

In November the weather pattern settled. Anticyclone conditions over the British Isles brought a state of high atmospheric pressure with an absence of weather fronts coming in from the Atlantic. This resulted in sheets of low cirrus cloud, mists, fog and drizzle. It was increasingly cold. As the month progressed, ops and training sorties continued but many were cancelled.

Winter fog was a worrying issue for Bomber Command. Beam Approach training, plus refresher courses, was one contribution to landing aircraft in such conditions.

A further development was the Fido fog-clearing system. This was to assist the increasingly large numbers of aircraft to land after a raid. So far, three installations were working: at Fiskerton near Lincoln; at Graveley near Huntingdon; and Downham Market in Norfolk, where the Fido runway ended half a mile short of the town.

Fido worked by pumping large quantities of petrol from storage tanks through small pipes laid parallel to the main runway. Petrol vapour emerging from holes at intervals was set alight, often by an airman riding a bicycle. Ten minutes after start-up, the heat from two walls of roaring flames lifted the fog enough for a pilot to see the runway. To reach this point he had to employ his Beam Approach training.

Each Fido operation used thousands of gallons of petrol. Making a landing in an aircraft using a Fido runway for the first time was a dramatic – even awe-inspiring – experience.

The weather in November was generally poor and Ernest Deverill carried out only one or two fighter affiliations.· Meanwhile the wheels of Bomber Command administration were turning to recall him from his "rest" in AFDU. On November 21 he was attached to 1660 Heavy Conversion Unit, also at Swinderby, to crew up for a return to operations.

Next day he borrowed one of the Spitfires to make a return flight 80 miles south to RAF Bourn near Cambridge. His old unit, 97 squadron, was now based at Bourn since its transfer to 8 Group, Pathfinder Force in April. That one-day visit was taking him back to squadron life.

On November 24 he recorded his new crew in the logbook:

Lancaster LN 309 Self, F/Sgt Farr, F/Sgt Russell, P/O Brown, W/O Benbow, W/O Penfold, F/Sgt Crossgrove. First flight of 1hr 35 mins.

They made more flights in the next few days, including a cross-country and night affiliation exercise, to work up as a crew. On December 4, the HCU's chief instructor signed Ernest's logbook for the month of November. Whether he had any leave before his new posting is not known, but it must have been two days at best.

All but one of the crew were British. P/O John Brown, the navigator, 22, was from Belfast in Northern Ireland. Flt Sgt Alexander Russell, flight engineer, came from Epsom in Surrey, Flt Sgt Francis Farr, the bomb aimer, from Windsor, in Berkshire. At 19, he already had completed a tour with 106 Squadron. He was the youngest crew member.

Flt Sgt Ralph Crossgrove, 25, the wireless operator, of the Royal New Zealander Air Force, won the DFM while on Lancasters with 57 Squadron. Married, he had left home in Auckland, and his wife Bessie, to join up shortly before their child was born, in April 1941. However, the boy he had not seen had died aged two.

Jim Benbow, Deverill's mid-upper gunner from 1942, had since been promoted to warrant officer. He heard that his old skipper was returning to ops and was keen to fly with him again. At 35 he was the oldest crew member. The rear gunner, Warrant Officer Donald Penfold, came from the South Coast town of Worthing.

Now, 97 Squadron was one of the eight Pathfinder squadrons, a force of heavies and Mosquitos. Pathfinders were the specialists whose aircraft dropped target indicators (TIs), pyrotechnic marker flares (skymarkers and ground markers) ahead of the main-force aircraft to help them bomb accurately. Ernest Deverill would again be at the centre of events in the bomber war.

A Pathfinder tour was 45 ops instead of the normal 30. However, Pathfinder aircrew were each given an automatic promotion on being posted there. Deverill, therefore, returned to his old unit with the rank of acting squadron leader. This required adding a thin "scraper ring"[96] to his tunic sleeve, between the flight lieutenant rings.

His pay went up accordingly, the basic rate rising from £1 1s 9d a day to £1 10s 10d. But his life, and lives of his new crew, were in the hands of Harris and Bennett, the unknowns of H2S – and the weather.

PATHFINDERS

It was well known that Air Vice-Marshal Donald Bennett, who commanded 8 Group from the fine 18th century Castle Hill House in the town of Huntingdon, was a quite exceptional airman. Bennett, who grew up living a rugged outdoor life on an Australian cattle station, had an astonishing CV. After joining the Royal Australian Air Force, then the RAF, he amassed a wealth of flying experience, and was a master navigator.

In the mid-1930s Don Bennett had written a standard textbook, *The Complete Air Navigator*, a title that was no exaggeration since it had many pages explaining astro navigation. Before the war, he captained flying boats for Imperial Airways on routes across the Pacific.

He returned to the RAF during the war and was shot down piloting a Halifax over Norway while attacking the battleship *Tirpitz*. Remarkably, he and his wireless operator walked across Norway to reach neutral Sweden and got back to England in only a month. At 33 he was the youngest air vice-marshal in the RAF.

Most unusually for a senior officer, Bennett held a sheaf of technical qualifications: flying instructor's certificate, wireless operator's licence, and three categories of ground engineer. Even his movements in the cockpit, while carrying out the procedure to start up an aircraft, were a model of economy. All this gave him an unnerving ability to ask searching technical questions when visiting his stations.

One of his station commanders was "Honest John" Searby. Since March 1943, Searby, who had joined the

RAF as an apprentice, was moved on swiftly from C.O. at 106 Squadron to command 83 Squadron at Pathfinders, then made "stationmaster" at two of Bennett's stations. Searby described Bennett as "a ready listener with a good sense of humour but it is true that he had no use whatever for place-seekers, pompous individuals or time-wasters".[97]

Navigation was "the name of the game" in Pathfinders, both to arrive at the target exactly on time and to reduce losses from aircraft straying over heavily defended areas. The group had its own navigation school for new crews.

In November 1943, Pathfinders switched to measuring speed and distance in knots, instead of miles per hour and miles, so that the calculations by navigators would be more accurate. When 97 Squadron arrived at 8 Group, in characteristic style Bennett told the assembled airmen that pilots were "merely chauffeurs to get the really important people, navigators and bomb aimers, to the right place to drop their TIs, flares and bombs".[98]

The AOC's perfectionist standards and direct manner did not win him friends easily, but he had able lieutenants to manage the day to day work, from administration to aircraft maintenance schedules and recruitment. One of these was Wing Commander "Hamish" Mahaddie, 8 Group's Training Inspector. He, like Ernest Deverill, was a former apprentice and old "Mespot hand".

Mahaddie's rank, generous rows of medal ribbons on his tunic and breezy Scots manner opened the doors to messes, briefings and group commanders' offices. While his visits officially were to give lectures on bomber tactics, this was a polite cover that enabled him to poach the best crews for Pathfinders, having studied their aiming-point photographs.

Individuals in new crews who made the grade were awarded the gilt Pathfinder badge, depicting an eagle in flight. These awards, with a certificate, were approved by Bennett in batches.

Ernest Deverill, well known in the Command, will have entered Pathfinders on the say-so of Mahaddie since it was judged time was up for his "rest" at AFDU. Indeed, vacancies from the steady losses had to be filled.

Very likely, the new squadron leader was keen to get back on ops, the aim of many bomber men who missed the camaraderie of squadron life. And so Deverill's crew were added to the names on the large board in Mahaddie's office.

The new crews were assessed over their first dozen or so trips to confirm they met Bennett's high standards. Then they could be given target-marking responsibilities.

With operations halted by the foggy weather since he arrived, Sqn Ldr Deverill may have visited Castle Hill House to meet Mahaddie, or summoned for a chat with Bennett. Thus entering the atmosphere of a bomber group headquarters with its "air of quiet, cold efficiency... The yellow lights over the AOC and SASO's[99] doors are almost always on, showing that they are engaged. Great decisions are being taken the whole time," as Gibson at 5 Group observed.[100]

Many of Bennett's absences from Castle Hill House through the summer and autumn of 1943 had been to work with scientists on much-needed changes to H2S. First, the "boffins" produced a Mark 11 version, which had a number of improvements.

Two main problems remained however: the fuzzy image reflected from ground features, and the image on the navigator's display falling off the screen when the aircraft rolled.

In late summer, a radical change was made to the

operating wavelength, from 10cm to the narrower 3cm, to achieve better definition. This involved extensive redesign of the electronic circuits and other parts. The boffins also devised a gyro-controlled tilting frame for the scanner so it maintained a vertical axis during a roll, stabilising the image on the screen.

The 3cm Mark 111 was a dramatic step forward. Flying trials over British towns demonstrated that the new wavelength would display a difficult target such as Berlin in much better detail, and from a bombing height of 20,000 feet. These much-improved sets were badly needed for the raids against the Big City that Harris was known to be planning, but there was no hope of factory production starting in time.

With a quiet nod from Harris, Bennett and the H2S team agreed to bypass official channels. It was decided to hand-build a small number of sets in as short a time as possible. A deadline was set: to have Mark 111 sets installed in six Lancasters by mid-November.

On November 11 the scientist Bernard Lovell wrote in his diary: "Tremendous pressure on our six Lancs. I have a feeling that B.C. [Bomber Command] are about to make an all-out effort on Berlin. I told Bennett last night that we'd try to deliver three on Sunday and three on Tuesday."[101]

Six new Lancasters fitted with 3cm sets were flown in to 83 Squadron at RAF Wyton between November 13 and 17 and put in the hands of the most experienced crews. Harris restarted the raids on Berlin the next night. However, the important roll-stabilisation feature was missing because the special tilting frames were not available. Nor were the sets reliable yet.

The Wyton pilots were instructed to turn back from

an op if their H2S was u/s when they reached the Dutch coast. This was to try to prevent one falling into enemy hands. Meanwhile, the squadron engineering officer and his radar mechanics were fully occupied keeping the new sets serviceable.

As thick cloud blanketed northern Europe, the success of the Berlin campaign depended even more on these new sets. Bomber crews knew well enough they would be sent back time and again until truly devastating results were achieved. As a Canadian pilot at Wyton put it: "I got the distinct impression that the equipment was more valuable than I was."[102]

Cloud over Berlin was making it impossible for reconnaissance Mosquitoes to obtain photographs of the damage the raids were causing. However, on the morning of November 25, readers of *The Daily Telegraph* picked up their paper to find a vivid eye-witness account of the aftermath of the bombing two nights earlier. Ossian Goulding, the Telegraph's correspondent in Stockholm, reported an interview with a Swedish businessman with "red-rimmed eyes and white, lined face" who had just returned from Berlin by air. The businessman said:

When I left this afternoon fires were still spreading in the centre of the city all round from the north to the south-west. The fire brigades and ARP personnel are powerless to cope with the situation. Day has been turned to night by the billowing clouds of evil-smelling smoke which fill the streets. The sky is blotted out.

The administrative heart of Berlin is paralysed. The Propaganda Ministry and Ministry of Munitions are badly damaged... The Foreign Office in the Wilhelmstrasse is wrecked, I

watched its evacuation this morning. Great lorryloads of documents, escorted by armoured cars, were continually leaving.

The Wilhelmstrasse and Unter den Linden districts are blazing so fiercely that firemen have given up the hopeless struggle. They have cordoned off whole blocks of buildings and simply left them to burn themselves out.

THE BIG CITY

It was misty and very cold when Squadron Leader Ernest Deverill reported at RAF Bourn on Monday December 6 to rejoin 97 squadron. The weather was "unfit for flying", the station log recorded, so airmen were kept occupied with ground training and lectures.

Bourn, on high ground a few miles west of Cambridge, had the familiar look of a wartime-built station. Joan Beech, a WAAF in the meteorological section, recalled: "At first sight the place seemed to consist of a huddle of rounded Nissen huts with cinder paths leading here and there… There were puddles everywhere, and a few grey-blue figures squelching from one hut to another."[103]

Of the Pathfinders' seven airfields, it was not the only one to fit this description. A visitor to Wyton, 10 miles away, said it was "as ugly as a wartime military base can be. Endless puddles, barracks, warehouses full of bombs, rusting wreckage of damaged equipment not worth repairing."[104]

At Bourn, Deverill found men he knew from his 1942 days at Woodhall Spa. However, those he had flown with were no longer there. The C.O. was now Wing Commander Noel Fresson, known on the squadron for his driving personality. He had recently earned an immediate DFC – and the nickname "Press On" Fresson – because of his determination to reach the target after flak badly damaged his aircraft.

Deverill's crew were put in B Flight and allocated Lancaster O-Orange, but the prospect of flying was uncertain because of the weather. By rank Deverill was effectively the new deputy flight commander with tasks to take on in the Flight office. B Flight's commander was Sqn Ldr Eric Cawdery, an "old man" of 31 who had taken over just days earlier after his predecessor failed to return from Berlin.

The Squadron was now flying Mark 111 Lancasters. These differed from the 1942 machines in having American-made Packard Merlin engines with fuel-injection carburettors offering better fuel economy. Petrol consumption was a big issue on long trips because, to carry more bombs, the permitted take-off weight for Lancasters had been raised to 65,000lbs, overloading them by 3,000lbs. Petrol load had to be carefully juggled against bomb load.

Problems were piling up for the bomber crews as winter advanced. Icing up in cloud causing loss of lift was increasingly likely. The H2S scanners had been freezing up in the bitter temperatures at 20,000 feet. To solve this problem Bennett ordered a mod, instructing ground crews to fit a pipe that directed hot air from the aircraft's heating system into the scanner housing.

Opposition from the German defences was relentless. The attack on Berlin of the night of December 2/3 was dramatically described in a radio broadcast to an American audience by Ed Murrow of CBS News. He gave a vivid report, from London, on his trip with a Lancaster crew, when "some of the young gentlemen of the RAF took me to Berlin".

Approaching the target, Murrow told his listeners, bombers were shot down, flak burst close. His aircraft had a near-miss with another Lancaster and it was coned by searchlights, corkscrewing to escape. Over the capital he saw fires from the bombing spread across the city. "The work that was done last night was a massive blow of retribution… Berlin was a kind of orchestrated Hell, a terrible symphony of light and flames," he said.

Joan Beech wrote: "Lancaster crews hated going to Berlin. It was simply too far and too spread out. Before a Berlin run the crews were always very subdued, and when they came back they were exhausted, if they came back."

Further, 97 Squadron was bearing its share of Bomber Command's rising losses: 11 aircraft and their crews had been lost on ops since the beginning of October – half its strength. The squadron had last operated on the night of December 3/4, pushing into Germany to bomb Leipzig through thick cloud. The marking by 83 Squadron, using their 3cm H2S, proved very accurate and the raid rated a great success. But again a B Flight aircraft of 97 Squadron did not return.

With low cloud, mist and fog preventing flying after Deverill's arrival, the squadron operations log filled with stand-down entries. The daily ops notification from Group clattered out of the teleprinter usually between nine and 10am. The record in the log read:

7.12.43 09.10 Ops Stand down. All squadrons make & mend. Station and navigation officers attend conference at HQ.
8.12.43 09.50 Ops Stand down
9.12.43 09.05 Ops 97 Squadron not required tonight
10.12.43 09.45 Ops Stand down

At Wyton on December 10, 83 Squadron's log recorded the general frustration: "What damnable weather, the damp and fog still persists." Snow showers the next day only added to the mood.

As at the other Pathfinder stations, crews at Bourn found their time filled with ground training, lectures and recreation activities. Off-duty, they could go to a station dance, or by bus or motor transport into Cambridge city centre with its pubs and Rex Ballroom. The most popular pubs were The Criterion and Baron of Beef.

11.12.43 09.45 Ops Not required tonight
12.12.43 09.50 Ops 97 Sqdn not required
tonight
13.12.43 09.45 Ops 97 Sqdn not required
tonight

On December 12 the weather improved, with moderate to good visibility. Deverill's crew went up at last. In O-Orange they carried out a cross-country flight of 1 hour 40 minutes. Next day they went up twice, for 2 hours 15 minutes and 3 hours 15 minutes. This was both to get their hand in and practice with the standard H2S equipment.

The weather worsened again over the next two days with mist and fog, so cross-countries were scrubbed and Deverill's crew stayed on the ground:

14.12.43 10.05 Ops 97 Sqdn not required tonight.
Make and mend
15.12.43 09.45 Ops 97 Sqdn not required
tonight

On December 15, Wing Commander Fresson was posted and Sqn Ldr Charles Dunnicliffe took over as Acting C.O. promoted to wing commander. Dunnicliffe, a former apprentice, knew the form because he had taken part in both the Leipzig and latest Berlin raids. However, Deverill's men, though experienced, had to get by with their limited flying time together as a crew. Ten days had elapsed since the last op and all on the station were aware that Harris would restart the Berlin offensive as soon as possible.

The teleprinter chattered as usual on the morning of Thursday December 16 and this time ops were "on". The weather team looked doubtfully at a synoptic chart that offered no change in the next 24 hours. The battle order went up with 21 crews listed, Sqn Ldr Deverill's among them – a maximum effort. The camp stirred into purposeful activity to prepare the aircraft, crew briefings, meals and transport.

Deverill was taking a different aircraft, P-Peter (JB243), for the trip. This was a fairly new Lancaster whose regular crew were on leave. He took P-Peter up for a 20-minute night flying test, then handed the Lanc over to the ground crew at dispersal to be fuelled and bombed up. By late morning the timetable was set, with the many station tasks required to get the aircraft on their way being carried out. Briefing for navigators would be at 13.30 hours, main briefing at 14.00, flying meal in the mess at 14.45.

Buses taking crews from their mess to the flights, to change into their flying kit, would leave half an hour later. Coffee and biscuits in the debriefing room on their return would be laid on from 22.30.

Yet conditions did not improve and many expected the op would be scrubbed. The state of the weather was confirmed by a pilot who landed late morning. He reported to Control that he had flown back from the coast at only 500 feet because of the low cloud.

When the curtain was pulled back at main briefing the 150 men saw immediately that the ribbon on the wall map led to Berlin. Zero hour was 8pm. Adding to their apprehension, the route across Germany was as before, a familiar direct route east, giving the defences ample warning.

The return route this time was a long leg North-West by North from Berlin, across Denmark to the North Sea. This would use more petrol but there were reasons for this track. A three-quarter moon would rise at 8.30pm, making the force visible to fighters above the cloud. The plan was to get the bomber stream to the target as quickly as possible, then avoid crossing north-west Germany and Holland when the moon was up. It was hoped that fog in north Germany would make conditions difficult for the night fighters, even keep them on the ground.

Officers in turn went through their briefings. Yellow route markers would be dropped to guide the bombers across Germany. Blind target marking would be used, dropping parachute flares from above the cloud, a method code-named Wanganui,[105] Eight primary and backer-up aircraft would drop red and green target indicators.

P-Peter carried bombs only since its crew, new to Pathfinders, were flying as one of the 13 Supporters, to start the bombing when the flares went down. There was risk of icing in cloud on the way, the met man explained. He spoke "at some length" of fog back at base later, but this would likely be after they returned. It did not look good so there was every chance the raid would be scrubbed.

Seven miles away at Graveley, the briefing for 35 Squadron, Pathfinders flying Halifaxes, was in progress. Sitting in the briefing room was Flt Lt Michael Allen, a Mosquito navigator from 100 Group. He had flown in from Norfolk with his pilot in an Oxford that afternoon to find the weather "closing in fast". "Suddenly, a messenger arrived on the platform and passed a note to the Briefing Officer, who paused in mid-sentence. Then: 'OK, chaps – ops are scrubbed for all Halifax squadrons, the Lancs are still going'. There was a mighty cheer!"[106] The risks to the Halifaxes of icing up in cloud were too great, the Lancs had a better chance. So it was now an all-Lancaster raid, close to 500 aircraft, with Mosquitos marking the target.

A quiet night could be expected at Graveley with the station on stand down. Aircrews likely would have a party or visit the public houses. At Bourn, the crews faced a hazardous return to ops, while for Deverill's crew it was a daunting start to their tour.

The thundering roar of 21 Lancasters warming up, taking off in turn and gaining height, filled the aerodrome and villages around Bourn. At 4.45pm P-Peter was fourth to become airborne and all were up by 5pm. They set course to leave the English coast at Southwold. As the sound of engines faded there was little for personnel on the station to do but wait.

The first aircraft to return was M-Mother flown by the Canadian Pilot Officer Snell. He landed at 11.25pm after 6hrs 45mins flying time. Second back, 25 minutes later, was Flight Lieutenant Wilson's Z-Zebra, scraping in, literally, when the starboard fin and rudder struck the runway as Wilson struggled to reach it in thickening fog.

In debriefing, they reported that fighter attacks began at the Dutch coast, the fighters dropping flares to light the bomber stream. The raid appeared to be successful.

The return at 12:05 of V-Victor, piloted by Flt Lt Charles Owen, showed what the crews were up against. Owen consulted his crew via the intercom on the options as they circled in the murk with increasing concern, and lost radio contact with Bourn Control. Then he made a decision. He wrote later in his diary:

Homed on to base on SBA bearing breaking cloud at 250 feet to find fog, rain and visibility about 300 yards and deteriorating. R/T then packed up, so after circling for 10 mins at 200 feet landed without permission in appalling conditions.[107]

The approach needed help from Owen's flight engineer, Sgt Lacey, to find the flarepath, recalled Sgt Leak, the bomb aimer. Owen sideslipped the Lancaster on to the runway "and we got down with a terrific bump and shot up in the air, but it was the best landing we ever made".

Shortly before midnight, on the station commander's orders, Bourn began diverting its aircraft to Graveley. At two minutes past, Deverill in P-Peter, and C-Charlie, after calling up, were both instructed to divert there.

However, the cloudbase at Graveley was only 500 feet, with poor visibility below that. Nor was Graveley's Fido system lit. The timing suggests P-Peter spent about 45 minutes circling at Graveley, probably stacked with other aircraft at the regulation 500ft intervals as they waited their turn to land. But the fuel remaining in the near-empty tanks of P-Peter was being used up.

The order was given at Graveley to light its Fido. The flames reached full burn a few minutes before 1am, though smoke from the start-up had yet to clear. Lancasters were circling in the whole area, some perilously close to the ground, in chaotic conditions. At Graveley another order intervened. The watchkeeper's log records what happened:

At 00.51 P-Peter and J-Jig were instructed to divert to Wyton and Warboys as it was thought

**that conditions were better there. C-Charlie
said he had only 15 minutes' petrol left. He
was told to go to Warboys. At 00.57 an aircraft
crashed to the west of the airfield, then S-Sugar
was told to go to Warboys.**

**Meanwhile P-Peter returned saying, 'There's
no future at Wyton, can I have a crack at your
Fido?' He approached almost at right angles to
the runway. Just as it looked as if he was going to
touch down he opened up and then his engines
cut and he crashed into the bomb dump and
burst into flames.[108]**

Rescue crews got to the wrecked aircraft and put out
the fire without delay, but only the mid-upper gunner Jim
Benbow survived the crash, at 1.20am. He was taken to
Station sick quarters, then to the RAF Hospital at Ely
25 miles away for specialist care. He had serious injuries:
burns to his hands and face and a badly fractured leg.

AFTERMATH

The telegram from Wing Commander Dunnicliffe and delivered to North Farm was addressed to Mrs J Deverill. It read: "Deeply regret to inform you that your husband S/L EA Deverill lost his life as a result of air operations. Letter follows. Please accept my profound sympathy."

Joyce was unwell, probably with influenza since a flu epidemic across the country was at its peak. Dunnicliffe's letter, sent the next day, said in part:

Deverill had only just been posted back to this squadron and I was very pleased to have him... It is especially sad that he should be lost after completing a successful mission. He knew quite a few of the present members of the squadron and I am sure he was very happy to be amongst us. We are all very proud of his exceptional tour of operational duties.

Her husband's personal effects would be safeguarded, the letter said, "and will be dealt with by the Committee of Adjustment Officer".

It was a disastrous night for 97 Squadron. One aircraft was lost over the target and then four in crashes when the aircraft returned, killing 28 men. Seven were injured. Two pilots decided against attempting to land. Instead, they climbed to gain altitude where the crews took to their parachutes, landing safely.

Next morning, the squadron's losses began to sink in. The one cause for quiet cheer was the return of Flt Sgt Bill

Coates' crew in N-Nan. Coates, on his first operation, brought his Lancaster back "on two engines, both on port side, and all instruments u/s" after being set on fire by incendiaries falling from above then further damaged by flak. He put down at Downham Market, "effecting a masterly landing" amid the Fido flames. His determination earned Coates an immediate DFM.[109]

At Graveley, the Mosquito navigator Michael Allen learned the extent of the losses on and near the airfield. Writing later, he was matter of fact: "Some of the Lancs had tried to use the newly installed Fido system to get in at Graveley itself, but four crashed around the airfield attempting to make a landing off a normal circuit, instead of flying out on a reciprocal to the runway and carrying out the normal blind-approach procedure.

"The welcoming glare thrown up through the fog by the oil-burners set out along the runway was too tempting for some pilots and they were loath to leave it, even though it was much safer to do so. Rumour has it that there were 27 bodies in the station mortuary."[110]

At Bourn, an instruction was given in the early afternoon that all 97 Squadron's crashes should be searched "for escape aids and secret equipment". By 4pm the result came back: "Only maps and a few cartridges found. These fit only for destruction."

It had been a terrible night for Bomber Command. On the raid itself, more than 20 aircraft were shot down. Five crews that returned saved themselves by bailing out instead of landing. But many more bombers crashed in the fog, with many killed and injured, trying to land at airfields in Cambridgeshire, Lincolnshire and Yorkshire. Worst affected was 97 Squadron. The night was remembered as "Black Thursday".

The squadron was assembled and "Dunnicliffe came in with a very serious face and did a lot of straight talking", Tom Leak, Owen's bomb aimer, remembered. "He said: 'Well, men, I know how you are feeling about the events that happened and you've lost colleagues, and it was very unfortunate that the weather changed as it did and brought such tragedy.

'No doubt you feel indignant about it, you feel like going out and talking about it'. But he warned us that was the very thing the enemy wanted to know... We were told if anyone spoke about this to the public they were liable to a court martial."[111]

The administration work that followed 97 Squadron's crashes included completing a standard accident card for each aircraft lost. All those that tried to land at Graveley or Bourn but crashed had similar wording. The card for JB243 read the crash occurred "attempting to locate airfield in conditions of bad vis[ibility] & low cloud".

It recorded that the pilot was not using beam approach, that the accident resulted from the "pilot's E of J" (error of judgment). There was no mention of P-Peter having to circle until the petrol tanks were near empty.

Bennett scheduled a meeting for the following Sunday that, presumably, was intended to learn lessons from what had gone wrong. However, no written report appears to have resulted.

Ernest Deverill's funeral was held at the parish church in Docking on the morning of December 22, the same day as funerals for most of those lost from the squadron. The choir at St Mary's rarely sang at a funeral service but was brought in for this exceptional event attended by many local people. The choir filed into the churchyard with the funeral party to the graveside for the burial.

The funeral for his New Zealand wireless operator, Ralph Crossgrove, was held the same day in Cambridge at the City Cemetery. He was one of 20 airmen from the crashes who were laid to rest there that day.

On Christmas Eve, a Norfolk paper reported: "News of the death of Sqn Ldr E A Deverill DFC and Bar, DFM, which occurred while on active air operations, was received in Docking with deep regret... Popularly known as 'The Devil' by his comrades, he was something of a celebrity in the Service.

"The Burgis family is an old and well-known one in north-west Norfolk, and there will be an extensive circle of relatives, acquaintances and friends who will feel sympathy for the young widow in her bereavement."

On January 1 1944, it was announced that Flight Lieutenant Ernest Alfred Deverill DFC, DFM had been awarded the Air Force Cross. The medal was in recognition of Ernest's work commanding the fighter affiliation unit at Swinderby.

An official description explains the award was made "for acts of valour, courage or devotion to duty whilst flying by officers and warrant officers, but not in active operations against the enemy". The citation read:

This officer has been almost solely responsible for teaching tactics against fighters and his energies in organising the exercises and carrying them out in the air have been outstanding. He was responsible for forming the unit and obtaining the optimum conditions for this work. He has had remarkable achievements in the number of crews that have received instruction.

POSTSCRIPT

In December 1944, and for several years after, a notice appeared in the *Dover Express* newspaper placed by the Deverill family. It read: "In proud and never fading memory of Squadron Leader Ernest Deverill DFC and Bar, AFC, DFM in tribute to his gallant crew of Pathfinders."

The Imperial War Graves Commission (later the Commonwealth War Graves Commission), took on the care of his grave in the churchyard. The commission installed its dignified headstone, made of Portland stone. Carved on this was Joyce's chosen inscription, taken from the war poem *O Valiant Hearts*, by Sir John Stanhope Arkwright:

TRANQUIL YOU LIE
YOUR KNIGHTLY VIRTUE PROVED.
YOUR MEMORY HALLOWED
IN THE LAND YOU LOVED

Joyce commissioned a poignant memorial to her husband for St Mary's church. Two quatrefoil traceries, created by a stained-glass maker in Birmingham, portrayed an angel playing a musical instrument. The traceries were installed in the East window, with a brass plaque added on the wall below.

Jim Benbow, the mid-upper gunner, was a patient in the RAF Hospital at Ely for 11 months. Then he was transferred to the Queen Victoria Hospital at East Grinstead, Sussex, for operations on his burns under the care of Archibald McIndoe, the pioneering reconstructive surgeon.

As one of McIndoe's "Guinea pigs", he had a series of operations at the hospital. McIndoe's skills in the operating theatre were matched by his concern to keep up his patients' spirits by promoting a lively social atmosphere, to prepare the men for their future life.

Invalided out of the RAF in 1945, Jim Benbow returned to Middlesbrough and the cafe business with his wife Madge. However, he never fully recovered from his injuries and died in 1956 aged 47.

Times changed for the Deverill and Burgis families. During the war Ernest's father served at *HMS Lynx*, the shore base at Dover, then retired from the Navy in 1946 with the rank of Lieutenant Commander. He and Elsie moved to a village in Cornwall. In 1952 he died from a heart attack while digging a well in the garden. He was 64.

Doreen served as a Wren driver at *Lynx* during the war, leaving the WRNS as a Leading Wren in 1945. She joined her parents in Cornwall, where she ran a cafe. Doreen married but died young at 45 in Portsmouth.

Her brother, Dimps, saw action in the war as chief electrical artificer on destroyers and an aircraft carrier. After retiring from the Navy in the 1950s he entered the teaching profession. He died in 1996. Their mother, Elsie, swimming daily as the years passed, lived to 92.

Joyce was still living with her parents when the war ended. She had an RAF widow's pension of £70 a year. Her sister Rita, restless in Norfolk, initially found work in London as a children's nanny. Her ambitions worked out. In 1947 she married a City coffee broker, entering an affluent life that included black-tie dinner functions and foreign travel. John Burgis returned from the war, in which his tank regiment fought in North Africa, to find that prospects for taking over the tenancy of North Farm were not encouraging.

His father advised him: "There's no money in farming, better to do something else." Accordingly, John put his trade training to good use by opening a butcher's shop in a town in Suffolk, achieving steady success.

Richard Burgis continued his steadfast work for the community but during 1947 his health declined. Worsening heart trouble depleted him and on November 4 he died at home. He was 65. The funeral was very well attended, swelled by representatives of the many local organisations with which he was connected.

Joyce and Blanche were left at the farmhouse and this brought the farm tenancy to an end, and two centuries of Burgises at North Farm. Mother and daughter moved to Hunstanton and, in 1949, found a roomy Victorian house in a quiet street.

Living a few minutes from the seafront allowed them to enjoy walks on the promenade, and the spectacular sunsets over the Wash for which Hunstanton is known. Joyce would visit Docking to put flowers on Dev's grave, sometimes accompanied by a young niece.

She did not remarry but over the years kept occupied with quiet work in Hunstanton as a member of local organisations that included the Women's Institute, Flower Club and Conservative Association. Joyce gave to her church and visited people who were housebound, riding about the town on her bicycle. At intervals, Rita drove up from Surrey to collect Joyce and her mother, taking them to keep house while she and her husband were abroad.

Blanche died in 1977. Joyce carried on with the

charitable work and remained keen on tennis, following the big events on television.

In late June 1992 Joyce, at 75, was at home watching the Wimbledon Championships – Andre Agassi was making the breakthrough to his first Grand Slam win – when she had a fatal heart attack. Wimbledon was her favourite TV programme.

After the war, the village of Docking returned to the ordinary life of a farming and business community. As tractors took over the heavy work on the farms the number of heavy horses in the district dwindled until the last few "gentle giants" were sold in the 1960s. Most went to the knacker's yard. "They spent the night in the cart shed, they'd gone the next morning," a worker at North Farm remembered.

Portsmouth, so heavily bombed, was rebuilt in the 1950s after much indecision over the best way to re-plan the city. New homes, shops and roads filled many bomb site spaces. Roads were improved. A civic milestone was reached in 1958 when the burnt-out Guildhall was occupied again after a complete restoration. It was re-opened officially by the Queen the following year.

Chivers, the Southsea crammer where the young E.A. Deverill, and brother Derek, laboured to pass their apprentice exams, moved from the church halls to new premises and soldiered on through the 1950s. Two senior masters from Ernest's time still taught there. Chivers was passed by increasingly in the post-war years after the national school-leaving age at last was raised to 15 in 1947. The school struggled with a declining number of pupils until it closed in 1966.

HMS Vernon, the shore establishment in Portsmouth that Ernest's father knew so well, was sold off in 1996.

Developers transformed the site into a smart retail destination, Gunwharf Quays, offering shops, restaurants and bars. The main gate that torpedo officer Deverill walked through to work in the 1920s is today an entrance for shoppers.

"Trenchard's Brats" served with distinction during the war in large numbers, many serving as flight engineers in Bomber Command were lost on operations. A significant proportion were commissioned, many rising to the higher echelons of the service.

Former apprentices did indeed meet Trenchard's far-sighted aspiration of the 1920s: that a high standard of technical and educational training would make them useful citizens in civilian life. One, Thomas Lancashire, became an aircraft designer in America. Cliff Michelmore was a nationally known BBC TV presenter from the 1950s to the 1980s. Another "bright boy" who entered the Halton system between the wars was Frank Whittle, who invented and developed the jet engine while an RAF officer.

As for the political battle of the 1920s and 30s over providing a secondary education for all children, Professor Andrew Gamble, Emeritus Professor of Politics at Cambridge University, explained in 2011: "Rab Butler's 1944 Education Act was the response. Education was re-organised as a democratically accountable service, nationally directed but locally administered."

He went on: "The war created the opportunity for change... but education has always been a battleground, and policy is constantly changing. Eighty years after Tawney wrote,[112] the lines of social class are as visible as ever in English education."[113]

Many of the aerodromes Ernest Deverill flew from were closed after the war. Bircham Newton with its impressive pre-war buildings continued as an RAF station until the 1960s. It was taken over as a training site for the UK construction industry, tall cranes poking above the trees.

RAF Docking was closed soon after the war and returned to farmland, having acted as a temporary holding unit for airmen awaiting their demobilisation. A number of wartime Nissen huts remained in use into the 1950s as temporary housing for local council tenants.

Coningsby, where 97 Squadron was based before moving to Woodhall Spa, remains as an important RAF station in the jet age.

RAF Bourn, where Deverill's crew took off on their final flight, still has its main runway which, several times each year, has been used as the venue for a large open-air general market. Development plans to build homes on the airfield site rumble on. RAF Graveley returned to farmland, with nothing remaining of the runways that were so close, yet so far, for those in P-Peter in December 1943.

Woodhall Spa perhaps has fared most kindly. The aerodrome was sold off in the 1960s to become a commercial sand and gravel quarry for many years. In 2014, the site was purchased by Lincolnshire Wildlife Trust, helped by a successful public appeal for donations. The trust then remodelled it as a nature reserve, creating lakes, reed beds and restoring heathland.

The concrete main runway, from which 97 Squadron's new Lancasters roared upwards to take part in the Augsburg raid in April 1942, serves today as a place to walk in peaceful surroundings. Here, visitors can watch skylarks, owls and herons in skies where Ernest Deverill and many other brave airmen flew.

CHAPTER NOTES

1. From turpentine, the solvent with heavy fumes that oil painters use
2. £5 5shillings (£5.25)
3. Manual of Seamanship Vol 1 1908
4. GA (Hank) Rotherham, It's Really Quite Safe!
5. Bruce Taylor, The End of Glory
6. New Zealand History https://nzhistory.govt.nz
7. TE Wooden, Recollections of Esplanade House School
8. Mick Cooper's Chivers page
9. Ralph Wolton, IWM oral history
10. Portsmouth Evening News, August 12 1929
11. Dundee Courier, September 9 1929
12. Entry and Training of Aircraft Apprentices, Air Ministry Pamphlet 15
13. Hampshire Telegraph, June 19 1931
14. Ralph Wolton, IWM oral history
15. Hansard, November 6 1930. The school-leaving age was not raised until 1947.
16. Thomas Lancashire, A Trenchard Brat at War
17. Flight, October 4 1923
18. Tom Robinson, in Boys at Cranwell
19. Tom Robinson, in Boys at Cranwell
20. Boys at Cranwell
21. Flight, February 5 1960
22. Kay Carroll, Compass Course: Log of an Air Force Officer's Wife
23. Account by 'Min' Larkin
24. CMH Frere, Boys at Cranwell
25. CMH Frere, Boys at Cranwell
26. In Roll of Apprentice Names, RAF Cranwell
27. Young Men's Christian Association

28. Ewart Chorley, in Boys at Cranwell
29. Ewart Chorley, in Boys at Cranwell
30. T E Lawrence, The Mint
31. Letter to Trenchard, December 1928
32. In Joe, Autobiography of a Trenchard Brat
33. Kay Carroll, Compass Course
34. In GA Rotherham, It's Really Quite Safe!
35. Mornington Wentworth, IWM oral history
36. Air Power and Colonial Control, David Omissi
37. Article in Rolls-Royce Owners Club of
Australia magazine, 1980
38. RAF Armoured Car Companies in Iraq, Christopher
Morris
39. RAF Armoured Car Companies in Iraq
40. Stanley Eastmead, IWM oral history
41. Royal Air Force Armoured Car Manual 1931
42. PJP Trotman, J for Johnnie
43. Maurice Stretton, IWM oral history
44. David Ogilvy, article in General Aviation, August 2006
45. DCT Bennett, The Complete Air Navigator
46. John James, The Paladins
47. Murray Peden, A Thousand Shall Fall
48. Ralph Wolton, IWM oral history
49. John James, The Paladins
50. K6183 was shot down into the sea. Its pilot
survived and was taken prisoner
51. Ted Rayner, IWM oral history
52. Gron Edwards, Norwegian Patrol
53. Alexander Scrimgeour, Scrimgeour's Scribbling Diary
54. Air Raid Precautions Service
55. Change in the Farm, Thomas Hennell
56. Early Ringway, Raymond John Webb
57. Gron Edwards, Norwegian Patrol
58. Sqn Ldr Tom Dudley Gordon, Coastal Command at War
59. Boulton Paul later issued a modification, Mod.150,
for the Hudson turret. A lanyard was attached to the

hydraulic release lever. If the gunner was incapacitated a crewman could pull the lanyard from below to disengage the hydraulic power.

60. Western Morning News, July 10 1940
61. Lynn Advertiser, August 2 1940
62. Verrall Grimes, Docking oral history
63. Jack Currie, Lancaster Pilot
64. Flt Lt Leslie Baveystock, Wavetops at My Wingtips
65. Guy Gibson, Enemy Coast Ahead
66. Lord David Cecil, in Men of the RAF
67. Katharine Bentley Beauman, Wings on Her Shoulders
68. Men of the RAF
69. Lancaster Flying Trials, AVIA15/1565
70. Lancaster Flying Trials
71. Don Charlwood, Journeys into Night
72. Quoted in Into Thin Air, Nigel Press
73. Harry Yates, Luck and a Lancaster
74. In Group Captain John 'Joe' Collier, Simon Gooch
75. Pip Beck, Keeping Watch
76. Alan White, The King's Thunderbolts
77. In TV documentary
78. Rodley's account quoted in Spink medal sale
79. 97 Squadron Operations Record
80. Pathé News
81. Aircraftman Stephen Rew, IWM oral history
82. Quoted in The Thousand Plan, Ralph Barker
83. Sherwood survived being thrown from the cockpit into bushes or trees
84. Ken Bourne, IBCC oral history
85. Guy Gibson in Enemy Coast Ahead
86. Report in Canberra Times, Oct 20 1942
87. Sqn Ldr Corr's Lancaster crashed into a wood. The rear gunner, the sole survivor, was taken prisoner.
88. John Searby in The Everlasting Arms
89. Leonard Thorne, A Very Unusual Air War

90. Flt Sgt of 218 Squadron, BBC WW11 People's War A1940014

91. John Searby, The Great Raids: Essen

92. Account by Sybil Bannister in I Lived Under Hitler. German authorities estimated that 3,400 people were killed in the attack and 80 per cent of the built-up area destroyed, including 1,800 homes and five of the six largest factories.

93. In Terence Rattigan, Michael Darlow

94. Quoted in The Bombers, Norman Longmate

95. Freeman Dyson, Disturbing the Universe

96. From the oil-scraper rings on the pistons of aircraft engines

97. John Searby, The Everlasting Arms

98. Arthur Spencer, 97 Squadron navigator, IBCC oral history

99. SASO = Senior Air Staff Officer

100. Guy Gibson in Enemy Coast Ahead

101. Bernard Lovell, in Echoes of War

102. Walter F Thompson, Lancaster to Berlin

103. Joan Beech, One WAAF's War

104. Freeman Dyson, Disturbing the Universe

105. A city in New Zealand

106. Michael Allen, Pursuit Through Darkened Skies

107. Diary of Flt Lt Charles Owen

108. Graveley Operational Record AIR28/322

109. London Gazette, January 7 1944

110. Michael Allen, Pursuit Through Darkened Skies

111. Account by Sgt Tom Leak, bomb aimer in Owen's aircraft

112. RH Tawney, the social critic, wrote in 1931: "The hereditary curse upon English education is its organisation on lines of social class."

113. Taking social class out of the classroom, Prof Andrew Gamble, Times Literary Supplement 2011

BIBLIOGRAPHY

Michael Allen, *Pursuit through Darkened Skies* (Crowood Press) 1999

Sybil Bannister, *I Lived Under Hitler* (Penguin) 1995

Ralph Barker, *The Schneider Trophy Races* (Chatto & Windus) 1971

Ralph Barker, *Strike Hard, Strike Sure* (Pen & Sword) 2003

Ralph Barker, *The Thousand Plan: The First Thousand Bomber Raid on Cologne* (Airlife) 1992

Leslie Baveystock, *Wavetops at My Wingtips* (Airlife) 2001

Katharine Bentley Beauman, *Wings on Her Shoulders* (Hutchinson) 1943

Pip Beck, *Keeping Watch: A WAAF in Bomber Command* (Goodall) 1989

Joan Beech, *One WAAF's War* (Seven Hills) 1989

Gertrude Bell, *The Arab of Mesopotamia* (Westphalia Press) 2016

Kevin Bending, *Achieve Your Aim* (Woodfield Publishing) 2005

DCT Bennett, *The Complete Air Navigator* (Pitman) 1941

Don Bennett, *Pathfinder* (Goodall) 1998

Martin Bowman, *Bomber Command Reflections of War Vol 2, Vol 3* (Pen & Sword) 2012

Alan Bramson, *Master Airman: A Biography of AVM Donald Bennett* (Airlife) 1985

Kay Carroll, *Compass Course: Log of an Air Force Officer's Wife* (Hutchinson) 1941

Don Charlwood, *Journeys into Night* (Burgewood Books) 1991

WR Chorley, *RAF Bomber Command Losses 1942* (Midland) 2006

WR Chorley, *RAF Bomber Command Losses 1943* (Midland) 1996

Coastal Command, Air Ministry (Stationery Office) 1943

Jack Currie, *Lancaster Target* (Goodall) 1981

Jack Currie, *The Augsburg Raid* (Goodall) 1987

Michael Darlow, *Terence Rattigan* (Quartet) 2000

Hugh Dundas, *Flying Start* (Penguin) 1990

Freeman Dyson, *Disturbing the Universe* (Harper & Row) 1979

Gron Edwards, *Norwegian Patrol* (Airlife) 1985

Beryl Escott, *Women in Air Force Blue* (Patrick Stephens) 1989

David Fletcher, *The Rolls-Royce Armoured Car* (Osprey) 2012

Martin Francis, *The Flyer: British Culture and the Royal Air Force* (Oxford) 2011

Michael Frere, *The Cranwell Boys 1934-1940* (Acorn) 1999

Mike Garbett & Brian Goulding, *Lancaster* (PRC) 1995

Guy Gibson, *Enemy Coast Ahead Uncensored* (Crecy) 2003

Simon Gooch, *Group Captain John "Joe" Collier* (Pen & Sword) 2015

Cy Grant, *A Member of the RAF of Indeterminate Race: WW11 Experiences of a West Indian Officer* (Woodfield) 2012

Jennie Gray, *Fire by Night* (Grub Street) 2003

Jennie Mack Gray, *Ernest Deverill: A Knight of the Air* (RAF Pathfinders Archive) 2018

John Green and Robin Money, *Exploring the History of Lee-on-the-Solent* (Chaplin Books) 2013

D'Arcy Greig, *My Golden Flying Years* (Grub Street) 2010

Peter Gunn, *Bircham Newton: A Norfolk Airfield in War and Peace, 2002*

Sir Arthur Harris, *Bomber Offensive* (Pen & Sword) 2005

Andrew Hendrie, *Cinderella Service: RAF Coastal Command 1939-1945* (Pen & Sword) 2010

Andrew Hendrie, *Seek and Strike: Lockheed Hudson in WW11* (William Kimber) 1983

Thomas Hennell, *Change in the Farm* (Cambridge) 1934

David Jacklin, *Up in All Weather: The Story of RAF Docking* (Larks Press) 2004

John James, *The Paladins* (Sphere) 1991

John Kilbracken, *Bring Back My Stringbag* (Pen & Sword) 1979

Robert Kirby, *Avro Manchester* (Fonthill Media) 2015

Richard Knott, *Black Night for Bomber Command* (Pen & Sword) 2014

Max Lambert, *Night After Night: New Zealanders in Bomber Command* (Harper Collins) 2005

Thomas Lancashire & Stuart Burbridge, *A Trenchard Brat at War* (Pen & Sword) 2009

T E Lawrence, *The Mint*, (Penguin 20th Century Classics) 1978

Norman Longmate, *The Bombers: RAF Offensive Against Germany 1939-45* (Hutchinson) 1983

Sir Bernard Lovell, *Echoes of War: The Story of H2S Radar* (Adam Hilger) 1991

Michael Luke, *David Tennant and the Gargoyle Years* (Weidenfeld & Nicolson) 1991

W J Lawrence, *No 5 Bomber Group RAF 1939-45* (Cedric Chivers) 1970

Hamish Mahaddie, *Hamish: The Story of a Pathfinder* (Ian Allan) 1989

Leo McKinstry, *Lancaster* (John Murray) 2010

Ross McNeill, *RAF Coastal Command Losses 1939-1941* (Midland) 2003

Hugh Melinsky, *Forming the Pathfinders* (History Press) 2010

Martin Middlebrook, *The Berlin Raids* (Cassell) 2000

Martin Middlebrook, Chris Everitt, *Bomber Command War Diaries 1939-45* (Midland) 1998

Russell Miller, *Boom: The Life of Viscount Trenchard* (Weidenfeld & Nicolson) 2016

The Modern Boy's Book of Aircraft (Fleetway) 1931

Hank Nelson, *Chased by the Sun: Australians in Bomber Command* (Allen & Unwin) 2006

Joe Northrop, *Autobiography of a Trenchard Brat* (Square One) 1993

David Omissi, *Air Power and Colonial Control: The Royal Air*

Force 1919-1939 (Manchester University Press) 1990

Cuthbert Orde, *Pilots of Fighter Command* (Harrap) 1942

Dame Felicity Peake, *Pure Chance* (Airlife) 1993

Murray Peden, *A Thousand Shall Fall* (Canada's Wings) 1979

Humphrey Phillips, *A Thousand and One* (Bomber Command Books) 2017

John Deane Potter, *Fiasco: Break-out of the German Battleships* (William Heinemann) 1970

Nigel Press, *Into Thin Air* (Tucann) 2003

Henry Probert, *Bomber Harris, His Life and Times* (Greenhill Books) 2001

Sir William Rothenstein & Lord David Cecil, *Men of the RAF* (Oxford) 1942

Dudley Saward, *Bomber Harris* (Doubleday) 1984

Dudley Saward, *The Bomber's Eye* (Cassell) 1959

R A Scholefield, *Manchester Airport* (Sutton) 1998

Stewart Scott, *Airfield Focus 28: Swinderby* (GMS Enterprises)

Alexander Scrimgeour, *The Complete Scrimgeour: Dartmouth to Jutland* (Conway) 2016

John Searby, *Bomber Battle for Berlin* (Airlife) 1991

John Searby, *The Everlasting Arms* (William Kimber) 1988

John Searby, *The Great Raids: Essen* (Nutshell Press) 1978

Nevil Shute, *Slide Rule* (Vintage) 2009

Tony Spooner, *Coastal Ace* (William Kimber) 1986

Ted Stocker, *Pathfinder's War* (Grub Street) 2009

Mary Stocks, *Workers Educational Association: The First 50 Years* (Allen & Unwin) 1953

Charles Stokes, *A Century of Life* (Fastprint) 2013

Martin Streetly, *Confound and Destroy* (MacDonald) 1986

John Stubbington, *Bomber Command: Kept in the Dark*, (Pen & Sword) 2010

R H Tawney, *Secondary Education for All* (Labour Party/ Allen & Unwin) 1922

Walter Thompson, *Lancaster to Berlin* (Goodall) 1985

H Leonard Thorne, *A Very Unusual Air War* (History Press) 2013

Frank D Tredrey, *Pilot's Summer* (Tyger & Tyger) 2000

Nigel Warwick, *In Every Place: RAF Armoured Cars in the Middle East 1921-53* (Forces & Corporate) 2014

John Weal, *Aircraft of the Aces: Bf109 1939-41* (Osprey) 1996

Raymond John Webb, *Early Ringway* (Webstar Graphics) 1978

Jane Wellesley, *Wellington: A Journey Through My Family* (Wiedenfeld & Nicolson) 2008

Alan White, *The King's Thunderbolts, 44 Rhodesia Squadron RAF* (Tucann) 2008

Frank Whittle, *Jet: The story of a Pioneer* (Frederick Muller) 1953

Geoffrey Williams, *Flying Through Fire: Fido the Fogbuster of World War Two* (Grange Books) 1992

Steven Zaloga, *Defence of the Third Reich 1941-45* (Osprey) 2012

Adam Zamoyski, *Forgotten Few: The Polish Air Force in World War 11* (Pen & Sword) 1995

ROYAL NAVY

Henry Baynham, *Men from the Dreadnoughts* (Hutchinson) 1976

AGF Ditcham, *A Home on the Rolling Main: A Naval Memoir 1940-1946* (Seaforth) 2013

William Donald, *Stand by for Action* (Seaforth) 2009

Roxane Houston, *Changing Course: Experiences of a Member of the Women's Royal Naval Service 1939-1945* (Grub Street) 2005

Admiral Sir W M James, *The British Navies in the Second World War* (Longmans) 1946

Brian Lavery, *Hostilities Only: Training the Wartime Royal Navy* (Conway) 2004

Brian Lavery, Nelson's Navy: *The Ships, Men and Organisation* (Osprey) 2020

Stephen Roskill, *The Navy at War 1939-45* (Wordsworth)

G A (Hank) Rotherham, *"It's really Quite Safe!"* (Hangar Books) 1985

Bruce Taylor, *The End of Glory: War and Peace in HMS Hood 1916-41* (Seaforth) 2012

Ken Whitehead, Janet Chapman (eds), *Memories of the Battle of the River Plate* (D&J Press)

ARCHIVES

International Bomber Command Centre https://ibccdigitalarchive.lincoln.ac.uk

National Archives

AIR5/170 Notes on Air Control in Undeveloped Countries

AIR5/532 Arrangements for Schneider Trophy Contest 1929

AIR 8/12 Permanent Organisation of the Royal Air Force, Hugh Trenchard 1919

AIR 16/757 Augsburg raid 1942

AIR20/857 Standard Beam Approach Equipment and Training

AIR27/449 44 Squadron ORB

AIR27/766 97 Squadron ORB

AIR 27/1222 206 Squadron ORB

AIR28/322/325 Graveley ORB

AIR 28/330 RAF Hinaidi

AIR29/50 RAF Hinaidi, Palestine Emergency

AIR29/718 No.1 Radio School, Cranwell

AVIA15/1565 Lancaster flying trials

Imperial War Museum

Aircraftman Stephen Rew, oral history

Diary of Flt Lt Charles Owen

RAF Pathfinders Archive www.raf-pathfinders.com

Royal Air Force Museum, Hendon

Trenchard Museum www.trenchardmuseum.org.uk

97 Squadron www.97squadronassociation.co.uk/

FURTHER SOURCES

Aircrew Remembered http://aircrewremembered.com
A History of the Mau Uprising in Samoa, Royal New
Zealand Navy Museum
Air of Authority, A History of RAF Organisation
www.rafweb.org
Air Transport Auxiliary Museum https://atamuseum.org
Babylon City of Wonders, BBC World Service 2020
Mick Cooper's Chivers Page http://michaelcooper.org.uk
Design and Development of the Avro Lancaster (Royal
Aeronautical Society) 1991
Diaries of Stella Benson, Cambridge University Library
Docking Heritage Group: oral histories
Hermeina Elms, Eileen Wells, Docking: A Walk in Time, 2000
Brian Foss, British Artists and the Second World War,
University of London thesis 1991
John Gallehawk, Some Polish Contributions in the
Second World War (Bletchley Park Reports) 1999
Maurice Gould, Recollections of Esplanade House
School (Portsmouth History Centre)
Gerald Hagan, Dry Docking
Janine Harrington, RAF Docking & Bircham Newton
(RAF 100 Group Association)
Beatrice Harrison, The Cello and the Nightingales
(John Murray) 1985
S E Harrison, Tramways of Portsmouth (Light Railway
Transport League) 1963
Roderick Hill, The Baghdad Air Mail (Nonsuch) 2005
Eileen Hooton-Smith, The Restaurants of London
(Alfred Knopf) 1928
King's Regulations of the RAF 1928, 1943
David Jacklin, Former RAF Buildings 2019

Jack Lazenby, Serving at RAF Bourn www.bbc.co.uk/history/ww2peopleswar

A J Ludlam, RAF Cranwell Railway (Oakwood) 1988

Fin Monahan, Origins of the Organisational Culture of the Royal Air Force (Birmingham University thesis) 2018

Newspapers: The Daily Telegraph; Dover Express; Dundee Evening Telegraph; Falkirk Herald; Gloucester Citizen; Hampshire Telegraph; Nottingham Evening Post; Portsmouth Evening News

New Zealand in Samoa, https://nzhistory.govt.nz/politics

Pathé News

R C Riley, Old Portsmouth: A Garrison Town – Portsmouth Paper 76 (City of Portsmouth)

G A Rotherham, It's Really Quite Safe! (Hangar Books) 1985

Ivy Scales, Recollections of The Norfolk Hero, 2001 www.stanhoe.org

Royal Air Force Historical Society journals online

Schneider Trophy Contest 1929 Souvenir Programme

R A Scholefield, Manchester Airport (Sutton Publishing) 1998

Stewart Scott, Airfield Focus: RAF Swinderby (GMS) 1997

Janet Smith, Liquid Assets: The Lidos of Britain (Malavian Media) 2005

John Stedman, Portsmouth Reborn – Portsmouth Paper 66 (City of Portsmouth)

Mary Stocks, A Hundred years of District Nursing (Allen & Unwin) 1960

Anthony Triggs, Portsmouth Between the Wars, (Halsgrove) 1998

Anthony Triggs, Portsmouth Past and Present (Milestone) 1984

Voices from Docking, Recollections of a Norfolk Village (Docking Heritage Group) 2019

Colin White, Nelson's Last Walk (Nelson Society) 2005

T E Wooden, Memories of Esplanade House School (Portsmouth History Centre)

INDEX

ACKNOWLEDGEMENTS

It would have been impossible to write this book without generous help, guidance and support from many people – individuals, staff at museums, libraries and archives, historical societies and elsewhere. In particular I wish to thank:

Steve Alcock, manager of Solent Sky Museum; Helena Aldis, Roland Axman and Paul Hewitt of Docking Heritage Group; Kevin Bending, 97 Squadron historian; Mark Beswick of the Met Office Library & Archive; Helen Bolton at Portsmouth History Centre; Charles and Brygida Bourn; Peter Burlton, researcher of RAF Habbaniya Association; John Clifford, Tim Dutton of the Pathfinder Collection, RAF Wyton; Michael Cooper, Mick Cooper's Chivers page; Cassandra Cope of Royal Navy records; Mary Davies; Simon Deverill; Jenny Earp; The Rev Michael Frere, for patience with my questions about apprentice life; Jennie Mack Gray, of the Pathfinders Archive, for her valuable support; Sarah Gretton of the Ratcliffian Association; Francis Hanford curator, and volunteers, at the Trenchard Museum; Pam Holmes; staff at Imperial War Museum; Heather Johnson, archives curator at the Royal Naval Museum, Portsmouth; Amy Jones; Derek 'Min' Larkin of the RAF Historical Society, who patiently helped with many questions; Tony Leach gave long-running help with my research; Vic Ludlow of the Royal Air Force Signals Museum; Antony Ramm at Leeds Central Library; Mary Rose Rivett-Carnac of Art UK; Nick Stein; Maureen O'Sullivan, who read my various drafts; Tim Pierce, librarian at RAF College, Cranwell; Tony Pilmer of the National Aerospace Library;

Steven Potter; Helen and Roger Roberts; staff at the Royal Air Force Museum, Hendon; Rachel Shaw of Lincolnshire Wildlife Trust; Dr John Stedman, records supervisor at Portsmouth Libraries & Archives; Ian Strutt efficiently sub-edited the text; Peter Tilley, consultant curator at Gieves & Hawkes Archives, Savile Row; Terry White, curator of the RAF Regiment Museum; Les Whitehouse, Boulton Paul archivist; Michael Wynd, researcher at National Museum of the Royal New Zealand Navy.

THE AUTHOR

Michael Strutt has been fascinated by aircraft and the Air Force since he was young. He is a former Fleet Street journalist who worked as a sub-editor on the staff of The Daily Telegraph and Financial Times, then freelanced for the The Times, The Sunday Times and elsewhere. He has written for newspapers and magazines on subjects as diverse as design, travel and restaurants.